LIGHTS ALONG THE WAY

LIGHTS ALONG THE WAY

STORIES AND POEMS

BY

THE CREATIVE WRITERS' GUILD

OF

THE MEMPHIS STORY TELLERS' LEAGUE

Illustrations by Sarah Crenshaw McQueen

Creekwood Press

Library of Congress Catalog Card Number: 97-69698

ISBN 0-9652829-2-9

Published by: CREEKWOOD PRESS
Memphis, Tennessee
1997

Printing by Allan & Akin, Inc.
Binding by Southern Bindery, Inc.

Printed in the United States of America

To the spinners of yarns,
The tellers of tales,
And those who have kept alive
The art of story telling
through the years.

Table of Contents

INTRODUCTION	*Jim Gray*	11
LIGHTS ALONG THE WAY	*Anne H. Norris*	13
THE PAPERBOYS	*Madge H. Lewis*	15
TO CALIFORNIA IN A BOX	*Anne H. Norris*	21
ME AND WALTER	*Ethel Joyner*	26
TECUMSEH WAS HIS NAME	*Ruth Crenshaw*	29
AMAZING GRACE	*Madge H. Lewis*	31
APRIL'S FATHER	*Malra Treece*	33
REMEMBERING RUTH	*Madge H. Lewis*	36
THE FLIGHT HOME	*Anne H. Norris*	37
THE WINE LIST	*Ethel Joyner*	43
THE THIEF	*Ann J. Huckaba*	45
SATURDAY'S WOMAN	*Madge H. Lewis*	49
MILLICENT AND ME	*Faye Livingston*	57
HERALD OF SPRING	*Anne H. Norris*	64
THE AWARD	*Ethel Joyner*	65
DEATH AND THE CLEANING WOMAN	*Malra Treece*	71
THE RESCUE	*Ann J. Huckaba*	77
THE TABLE	*Madge H. Lewis*	81
THE FAMILY TREE CHALLENGE	*Ethel Joyner*	87
A HOUSE NOT HER OWN	*Anne H. Norris*	89
A TIME OF SACRIFICES	*Rita Bernero West*	93
BETWEEN THE GRACE NOTES	*Madge H. Lewis*	97
HARD ROCK	*Ethel Joyner*	107
MY HUSBAND, THE NEAT FREAK	*Anne H. Norris*	109

Table of Contents

MY SECRET GARDEN	*Ethel Joyner*	115
GRAN'MA'S BLUEBIRD	*Ruth Crenshaw*	117
ADELAIDE	*Ann J. Huckaba*	125
THE AGES OF WOMAN	*Madge H. Lewis*	129
THE COMING HOME DRESS	*Ruth Crenshaw*	137
POINT IN TIME	*Madge H. Lewis*	143
MISS BELLE OF HOOTEN HOLLOW	*Anne H. Norris*	145
MORTIMER THE MOUSE	*Ethel Joyner*	153
FATHER MURPHY'S HAT	*Madge H. Lewis*	157
THE PHANTOM AND THE GHOST	*Ethel Joyner*	169
LEAH'S LAMENT	*Ethel Joyner*	172
THE DENIAL OF SUE ANN	*Rita Bernero West*	174
WHERE'S MR. PURDY	*Anne H. Norris*	177
WHEN AUGUST TERRY HELD COURT	*Nelle Weddington*	181
BONNIE ROSE	*Anne H. Norris*	185
MUSIC AND THE SCENT OF LILACS	*Ruth Crenshaw*	193
THE TREASURE CHEST	*Anne H. Norris*	199
THE ALTAR SOCIETY MEETING	*Madge H. Lewis*	205
A GARDEN FOR MAMA	*Malra Treece*	213
AN IMPROBABLE WITCH	*Ethel Joyner*	221
MOVE OVER, DOLLY	*Ruth Crenshaw*	225
LULA BETTERBEE'S CHRISTMAS TREE	*Anne H. Norris*	235
ABOUT THE AUTHORS		241
ACKNOWLEDGEMENTS		246

INTRODUCTION

THE STORIES in this book will not be found on the pages of slick literary magazines. Nor should they be, because they are stories that have something of a dual personality. Many of them first took shape not in printed form, but as *told* stories. They came wrapped in the style, syntax and special eloquence that story tellers bring to an audience, and each narration had within it the point of view and intense personal interest that made it unique. They were individually presented and ultimately judged not only for their standards of content and plot, but for the unique voices that told them.

A story with that kind of history has a special place in the hierarchy of American literature. Since the modern short story evolved as a uniquely American form, its roots must lie deep in the long–running traditions of story telling that evolved from earliest days of human activity on this continent—stories that originated with the oral histories of native Americans, and then later from the parables and religious fables that arrived with settlers from Europe and Asia, and the repeated myths and memories of Africans who passed stories down from generation to generation and kept their traditions alive.

Anyone, therefore, who undertakes to write stories owes a great debt of gratitude to story tellers. Many a writer has been molded at the knee of a friend or family member who excelled in the art of story telling. Eudora Welty, for example, tells of her childhood in Jackson,

Mississippi, listening with rapt attention to conversations between her mother and other ladies of the neighborhood. As each woman took her turn telling her story, she would incorporate wonderful details of dialogue into the narration, carefully attributed with *"She said"* or *"He said"*—perhaps followed with *"And then I said"*—all of it woven together in an exquisite tapestry of rhetoric that created, within a child's imagination, an unforgettable picture.

Ask about a writer's literary origin, particularly one who writes good short stories, and he or she will likely tell you that tales from childhood somehow took root in the psyche and began growing there. From that fertile environment, and nourished by the writer's imagination, those childhood tales grew into stories in their own right. But they often went further than that. They regularly produced variations and hybrids that evolved into new and original stories.

So it is with many of the stories contained in this book. They are grounded in the lives of the authors. For some of the writers, all past or present members of the Memphis Story Tellers' League, it is the first time their stories have appeared in print. But the stories succeed because each author conveys to her work a unique element—a blending of the art and craft of writing with the personal voice and individual perspective of a story teller. And that is a combination that, we hope, will bring a special joy to the reader.

Jim Gray, Editor
Creekwood Press

LIGHTS ALONG THE WAY

Anne H. Norris

My mother told me stories
  As she tucked me into bed.
This was a nightly ritual
  Before my prayers were said.

In school I listened eagerly
  To stories my teacher told,
Of kings and queens and palaces,
  And knights in days of old.

My young imagination soared;
  I lived the stories heard.
I became a gallant warrior,
  Mighty giant, or tiny bird.

Throughout my adulthood
  Are stories of every kind;
Some read for pleasure only;
  Others enrich my mind.

Now within my golden years,
  Stories brighten every day,
Emerging from my memory—
  My lights along the way.

THE PAPERBOYS

Madge Lewis

FOR FIVE years immediately preceding World War II, my younger brother Jack and his best friend Bubba shared two paper routes. They threw *The Commercial Appeal* in the early morning and the *Memphis Press Scimitar* in the afternoon.

Money was scarce and my mother, a widow with six children, needed every dime she could get her hands on. Bubba, who lived around the corner from us, was an only child and, by our standards, was rich. He really didn't have to work but he wanted to be with Jack—they were that close. They shared everything, the good times and the bad.

Their morning route required them to get up at four a.m. and there was much scurrying around to get to the station on time, fold the papers and zip on Bubba's bicycle from one house to another.

They bragged about how expert they became at throwing the paper smack–dab in front of the door of each house. They did this from one bicycle, Jack driving in an upright position and Bubba perched behind him on the seat, throwing the papers. The bag that held the papers was unwieldy when they started on their rounds, so they worked out a plan where Jack had a bag hanging over his left shoulder and Bubba over his right. That spread the weight and this worked fine in their early years when they were thirteen or fourteen years old. By the time they reached fifteen, though, the weight on that poor bicycle got powerful heavy.

In the afternoon when they delivered the *Press Scimitar*, they reversed the procedure, with Bubba pedaling the bicycle and Jack throwing papers. Friday night was collection time. Jack took one side of the streets and Bubba the other. Everything was double time with those two. Somehow after they settled up, they managed to eke out enough money for streetcar fare to town, which was seven cents each way, and twenty-five cents for a Saturday afternoon movie.

Bulldog Drummond was the boys' favorite Hollywood character. They liked to imitate his accent and had memorized many of the lines from his series of movies. They spoke to each other in the gentlemanly British accent of their idol, pretending to be working on a case for Scotland Yard. They had the role of the ex-army officer, with a taste for intrigue, down to a fine point.

I tell you, watching those boys grow up was an adventure. They made everything fun, even going to school where they delighted in playing tricks on the nuns. They were handsome little fellows: Jack with his chestnut hair and freckles sprinkled across his mischievous Irish face, Bubba with dark hair that fell into a recalcitrant lock he continuously brushed away from his brown eyes. In our school several grades shared a study hall, and I was usually in the same room with them. I heard Sister Ermanelda say they would be the death of her, but I spied a twinkle in her eyes several times when she chastised them for giggling and disrupting her class.

They teased everyone, but their favorite target was a lady who was on their paper routes. She lived on Central, a long, rich looking street, and she was very hoity–toity. Her name–so help me–was Mrs. Drummond, and as far as anyone knew there was no Mr. Drummond.

On Friday nights after the collections were over, the money counted, and most of it turned over to their mothers, I could hear the boys whispering and tussling and I knew they were up to their regular Friday night trick. One of these evenings after everyone was in bed at our house and it was quiet as an empty church, I cracked the door open enough to hear what was going on with the two little monsters. I heard Bubba give the telephone operator a number and both boys chuckled at the sound of the phone ringing at the other end. Then Bubba, in a deep, man's voice, said in his best British accent, "Mrs. Drummond, is the Bulldog in?" Even in the next room, I could hear Mrs. Drummond berating them over the phone. Bubba dramatically replaced the receiver and the boys rolled on the floor, laughing riotously.

Finally, Jack managed to choke out the words, "What did she say?"

It took Bubba awhile to quit laughing as he slapped himself over and over on his thighs. "She said if she ever found out who we were, bothering her this way every Friday night, she was going to have us arrested. She was r-e-a-l mad!"

"She'll never find out. No one knows but us," Jack said.

But I do, I thought, in my older sister, bratty way. I could tell Mom and they would have to quit bothering that old lady. Then I remembered my little brother slipping me enough of his hard earned money last week so I could go to a movie, and I decided I'd wait till I got a little madder at him.

Jack and Bubba were thirteen years old at that time. When they were eighteen, they received their draft notices. For five years that lady had put up with their shenanigans every Friday night but it was about to come to an end, at least until the war was over. And she still didn't know who was making those calls!

The boys were scheduled to leave from Central Station Saturday morning and we threw a farewell party Friday evening—just the family, and Bubba, of course. We served pretzels and Goldcrest 51 beer. That was all we could get in those days. At bedtime each member of our family hugged the boys, admonishing them to be careful and to write often. Mom hugged Bubba just as hard as Jack and she went to her room trying to hide her tears.

I peeped through the door to watch the boys. Jack and Bubba were slapping each other on the back. "See ya' in the morning, ole buddy," Jack was saying.

"Yeah," Bubba replied. "We'll—we'll just pretend we're heading out on our paper route."

"Say, we forgot the most important thing, Bubba," Jack picked up the telephone and gave the operator a number he obviously knew by heart. Then that little devil packed all the mischief inside him into his words when the phone was answered. "Hi, Mrs. Drummond. Is the Bulldog in?"

From where I stood I could hear her shouting at him, probably reminding him it was midnight, threatening to call the police. Jack hung up quietly and for some reason he and Bubba didn't react in their usual way.

The months went by, the years dragged on. Jack and Bubba were separated for the first time in their lives. Jack was sent to the European theater and Bubba to the Pacific. The glorious day finally came when the war ended in both areas and a few months later the boys were home.

Bubba had lost a leg, and Jack's right arm–his paper-throwing arm–was in a sling. After we got over the first shock of seeing them with their injuries, happiness engulfed us on our first night together. They had aged but there was still the gleam of mischief shining from their eyes. We were having such a good time celebrating their return that we were surprised when Jack asked if I would drive him and Bubba on an errand—an errand of mercy, he called it.

At that moment I would have taken him to the moon. We piled into my ancient jalopy, Jack, with his good arm helping Bubba maneuver himself and his crutches into the front seat.

"Sis, drive us down on Central. We want to call on an old friend."

I turned in at the driveway as directed. I watched from the car as Bubba held onto the banister of the stairway with his left hand and hoisted himself up each step with the aid of one crutch. Jack followed, ready to assist him if he needed help, and handed him his other crutch at the last step. They walked onto the porch where they had thrown newspapers for five years. Jack seemed hesitant, almost reluctant, as he rang the doorbell.

A tall, slender, white–haired lady came to the entry, tentatively opened the screen door and slowly, slowly took in the sight of the two young veterans of war who stood before her.

Bubba cleared his throat and Jack, hanging his head, shuffled his foot on the mat. Then they both said, as though in one breath, "Mrs. Drummond, is the Bulldog in?"

Mrs. Drummond stepped out onto the porch. She peered through her glasses at them, a myriad of emotions playing over her face. After a moment she took them into her arms and held the two of them close to her, tears spilling down her cheeks onto their uniforms.

"God bless you boys," she said laughing and crying at the same time. "I've prayed for you every night since you left, asking God to bring you back alive. And do you know what? I prayed the hardest on Friday nights."

TO CALIFORNIA IN A BOX

Anne H. Norris

NO ONE except my brother–in–law Egbert would have even considered such an adventure. It was 1946, World War II was history, and gas was no longer rationed. Egbert had completed an overhaul job on his old Chrysler sedan and was certain the drive from Memphis to Los Angeles would be a snap.

My brother–in–law was not a detail man, but he could come up with some mind–boggling ideas, and this one was a prize–winner. The trip would be educational and so much fun, it should be enjoyed by more than just him and my sister and their three daughters, ages five, nine and eleven. At Egbert's invitation and insistence, my brother Adam, his wife and two young children were added to the passenger list. To even out the number, he invited me, a sixteen–year–old who had never been outside of Shelby County.

Always the optimist, Egbert was sure ten of us in one car would be no problem. He drew plans and set about to build a box for the trunk. "The box" extended about two feet beyond the trunk of the car. It had high sideboards and a like-size board across the protruding end. In case of a sudden stop, this hopefully would prevent whatever, or whoever, was in "the box" from landing on the highway. It should be noted that the network of interstate highways stretching across our nation today had not then been constructed.

Had my mother been living at that time, it is unlikely I would have been participating in this marvelous, educational trip. That is because my "box seat" likely would have been occupied by Mama, who was always ready for a new adventure. It was not too difficult to convince my 75–year–old father that this would be the opportunity of my life. I would be under the watchful care of an older brother and sister. What could go wrong?

I am not sure whether air–conditioners for cars had been invented back then. I only know that my brother–in–law's car didn't have one. What we had was a canvas bag that was filled with water and fastened onto the front of the car over the radiator. I think this somehow cooled the engine. It did nothing to cool the passengers.

Most of the time, two of my nieces and I rode in "the box." This was a lot better than being inside the car with four adults and three other children, which was necessary when we crossed the desert because the heat in the box was unbearable. When we rode in the box we would watch for oncoming cars and wave at those who peered at us in total disbelief. This did not meet with the approval of my brother-in-law, especially when cars got so close he feared for our safety should he have to make a sudden stop. The girls and I enjoyed the attention and could not understand how our waving and shouting could in any way create potentially dangerous travel conditions.

As might be surmised, with ten people in the car (one way or another) there was little room for anything else. The necessities, therefore, rode on top. This included assorted pieces of luggage (using the term broadly) and our camping equipment. It would be an understatement to say that we were on a limited budget. Egbert had figured exactly how many miles we would travel and how much gas would be needed. He did not anticipate any emergencies, but stressed that we could not afford to be extravagant in our spending.

Most nights we camped "out." That is "out" as *out in the middle of the desert*. My sister–in–law was scared of the little varmints that scamper about in the dark, so she opted for the back seat of the car. The littlest ones were bedded down on the front seat. The luckiest ones got the box, and the rest shared quilts spread on the ground. My sister usually made the morning campfire, sometimes from dried cacti, and the aroma of perking coffee would get the rest of us up and ready for another adventurous day.

We never stayed in any of those wonderful RV parks that are along the major highways today. Even had they been available back then, it is doubtful our RV would have been welcome. We did, however, stay in a motel about every third night. This was absolutely essential so that we all could take baths and laundering could be done. Due to limited space, we were permitted to take very few changes of clothing.

One of the places on our "must see" list was the Painted Desert. I remember it well. We were a little behind schedule that day because we had encountered a terrible desert sand storm. The highway suddenly disappeared under a blanket of swirling sand. With zero visibility, we had to sit in the car and wait out the storm. This was a most memorable experience. A hot July day in the middle of a desert. Four tired adults, five irritable children and one disillusioned teenager, all inside one car with the windows closed and no air conditioning. Not an adventure to be soon forgotten.

The storm having caused us to get off of our schedule, the sign pointing out the Painted Desert was almost a blur. "There it is, off to the right. Everybody get a good look," shouted Egbert as we sped on our way. We did, however, enjoy the wonders of Carlsbad Caverns. The price of admission evidently had been figured into our budget because we took one of the guided tours.

We spent two nights at Grand Canyon National Park, arriving there late one afternoon. The mule train which daily takes tourists down to the river at the bottom of the canyon and back, was sold out for the following day. No problem. The round–trip was only 14 miles. Egbert, Adam, my sister and I could easily walk that far if we got an early start. My sister-in-law volunteered to stay with the children. In retrospect, I can see that she made a lot of wise decisions.

At the crack of dawn, the four of us were ready to hit the trail. Not wanting to carry any unnecessary items, we each had a small water bottle and several lemons in our pockets. Although the temperature rose to around 100 degrees and the sand on the trail was several inches deep, going down wasn't too bad. We moved aside and waved as the mule train passed us going down. Later in the day we again moved aside and waved as the mule train passed us once more, on its way back up. We were still on the way down.

Giving us words of encouragement, some of the riders said they had left snacks for us at the rest area. What a treat when we finally got there! We cooled our feet in the clear water of the canyon river, rested awhile, and started the long, uphill trek back. The day that had begun so wonderfully now was ending with us still several miles below the park lodge where we had left my sister–in–law and the five children.

My sister's pace had slowed, but she walked on without complaining. I would walk a few steps and stop, certain I could go no farther. I was thirsty, hungry and tired. Egbert threatened me with tales of wild canyon animals that came out after dark and killed everyone they encountered. I was too tired to care. As darkness began to settle in, Adam decided to leave us and get back to the lodge as quickly as possible to let the park rangers know that we were still on the trail.

We saw nothing on the entire trip more wonderful than the sight of four park rangers coming down to meet us. Helped along by two of them, I managed to make the last mile. It was after we were back in the lodge that we learned it was a rarity for anyone to make the 14–mile trip on foot during the summer months.

Eventually we did reach the West Coast. Two days later we were headed back home. Our trip was a great success. Not only had we seen some of nature's most outstanding attractions; we had enjoyed the hospitality of California relatives, made lifelong friends along the way, and proved that ten people in one car can endure a 5,000–mile trip—provided they are adventurous, not claustrophobic, and don't mind traveling in a box.

ME AND WALTER

Ethel Joyner

IF MY confidence level had ever risen above zero,
I surely would have been a world–renowned hero.
That the world took no note, what a great pity!
I go to a fantasy world with my friend, Walter Mitty.

He greets me warmly, then takes me by hand,
And we journey together to a make–believe land.
A world where I can be more than "Queen for a Day,"
As awards and commendations keep coming my way.

I walk onto the stage to thunderous acclaim,
They are wildly cheering and calling my name.
I accept the award without shedding a tear.
My peers have voted me "Mother of the Year."

My emoting has caused the audiences to weep,
I'm compared to the incomparable Meryl Streep.
The theatre reverberates with one loud cheer,
I win the Oscar for "Best Actress of the Year."

They madly applaud my tango rendition,
And I easily win the dance competition.
Oh, the joy and happiness we two did share
When Ginger sat down, and I danced with Astaire.

My third dissertation earned high accolades,
Distinguished colleagues were lavish in praise.
With such an amazing intellect, it's easy to see,
It's a piece of cake to add another degree.

Award winning time has come to an end.
I'm back in the real world, and gone is my friend.
A flight of fancy has passed, and I must confess,
My sink is stacked with dishes; my house is a mess.

TECUMSEH WAS HIS NAME

Ruth Crenshaw

THERE he sat, propped up as high as the crank on his hospital bed would allow. Except for the absence of a feathered headdress, the ridiculous flowered hospital gown, and the droop of one corner of his mouth, he had the bearing of the great chief whose name he bore.

On admission he was diagnosed as having had a stroke, leaving his right side paralyzed According to the Indian "ward boys" who brought him to his room, he still had the strength of a wild stallion. He had become so agitated, the physicians decided to postpone the rest of the routine; the result—he still wore his trousers and probably his moccasins.

Not a sound had he uttered since he arrived. So, it was presumed he had lost his speech. There he sat like the great stone face, only opening his eyes when someone came near. Then, they flashed with vengeance, the light of stark hatred turning the dark brown to black.

No one had been able to do more than the essential care for him. He accepted a few bites of warm cereal and sips of water from the Indian nurse's aides. Even with his useless arm and leg, he made a bath without restraints impossible.

It was the third day that Miss Quigley was assigned to him. She was buxom, starched from head to toe, and determined. She had a pleasant enough face, framed by dark hair worn in a bun under her nurse's cap, and the carriage of a general in full command.

She knew of the problems with Tecumseh and the first duty on her list was getting him out of those leather trousers and giving him a thorough bath. Since she was from Minnesota, she believed that all things should be scrubbed to a shine.

I watched her enter Tecumseh's room with soap, sponge, and basin of steaming water. What happened next I can only surmise. A shrill squeal came from the room and then I heard, "Ya, ya, ya!" A loud crash was followed by the sound of a body hitting the floor.

Everyone who was free rushed in. There the patient sat, placid as ever. On the floor sat Miss Quigley in a most undignified position, completely unstarched by the water from the basin which had been flung to the far corner.

Old Tecumseh was discharged the next day to be rehabilitated at home—with his dignity still intact and still wearing the leather trousers.

AMAZING GRACE

Madge H. Lewis

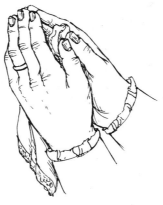

I SEE her for the first time in twenty-five years. She walks with a cane. That should not surprise me. She must be in her eighties, but is still tall and erect. I suppose I always thought of her as invincible, immune to the frailties of other mortals.

Strangely, the limp enhances her aura of dignity as each movement forward seems to be, not the beginning of a walk, but the first step of a graceful minuet. She holds her head high like a dowager queen poised for the proper placement of a tiara. Distress is betrayed by the merest tremble of a nerve beside her mouth. Her grey eyes are fixed upon the Italian marble of the altar as she advances slowly down the middle aisle of the church behind the coffin of her husband. The congregation stands in deference until the pallbearers come to a stop and the family is seated in the front pew.

I am touched by the beauty of the Requiem mass, the shadowy, quiet atmosphere of the historic old church. She is not a Catholic and he has not been a practicing Catholic for over forty years before his illness. But, with her usual sense of rightness, she has arranged for him to be buried in the church of his youth.

The priest delivers an eloquent eulogy describing the deceased as a virtuous man, loved by all who knew him, and generous to the worthy charities of Memphis. He tells us of the suffering the dear departed has endured during the last year of his life, bedridden and fearful of what the next world held in store for him.

At intervals during the service the hymns with organ and choir soar throughout the domes and rafters of the basilica. The mass comes to an end, not in the ancient way with the Latin words *Ite Missa Est*, but with a nod by the priest to the funeral director. The coffin, covered by an embroidered pall, is once again wheeled down the middle aisle.

She follows immediately behind, assisted by the strong arm of a young grandson. During the procession, the final walk, her face betrays a grief undisclosed throughout her sixty years of marriage. As I observe, I do not wonder about her sadness. Her expression surely is not for the death of this man so praised and eulogized by the priest, but for the lonely nights, the lost years when his blatant infidelities would have vanquished the spirit of a lesser wife, when his utter, all consuming selfishness denied her the love and tenderness of a faithful husband.

The whisper of the past vanishes from her face. I see her gather strength, head held even higher, step a little firmer, to complete the commitment she made sixty years ago.

APRIL'S FATHER

Malra Treece

ONCE upon a time and not too long ago, Herbert S. Billingsley, III, was acknowledged to be the neatest man in his neighborhood, no doubt the neatest in the entire city, state and universe. Along with neatness, he also liked quiet and peace, and a regular, dependable routine. He believed in order and stability. Some people considered him dull, but he did not mind, for he always knew where everything was stored, he never lost his glasses, and each month his checkbook balanced with the bank statement, to the penny.

He insisted that all the beds be made with military precision as he had learned to do in the Navy, with the sheets pulled tight, the corners tucked with three neat folds. Because his wife and children never made the beds just right, he was forced to do them himself. And no member of his family would ever place the dishes in the dishwasher as he knew they should go, or stack them neatly on the shelves, so he had to do these tasks, and many others, all alone.

His greatest difficulty was with the lawn, or what his wife called their garden. She was always planting vines that sprawled and flowers that left unsightly seed pods and bulbs that produced stalks that stood there doing nothing for weeks, then fell over and turned yellow, when he was finally allowed to cut them.

He planted the shrubs in front of his house in precisely straight lines. He sheared them into smooth, round balls, each the exact size of the other, measuring them with a yardstick as he pruned. He cut down the old magnolia tree (while his wife was away) because it was always dropping things. Magnolias do that. He cut the oak in the back yard because it shaded the vegetable garden, also planted in straight rows.

In his office he kept on his desk a telephone, note pad, pen, and his name plate. Nothing else was allowed except for the folder he held in his hands.

Their two sons married quiet, dependable girls and settled down to orderly desks and neatly made beds.

Their third child was different. She had arrived inadvertently, because of his wife's forgetfulness, sixteen years after the birth of their second son. His wife, illogically, he thought, named her April.

April kept her room in disarray and cluttered the house with her guitar, watercolors, poems, and laughing friends. She grew prettier each day, a fact that he somehow resented. Sometimes she hugged her father, although she knew that he did not like a display of emotion.

Because April's father took care of folding and stacking and putting things away, his wife sold real estate. She became so successful that she bought a more expensive house with a larger lawn, a swimming pool, and two dishwashers.

April's father was profoundly disturbed when his daughter moved into an apartment with her young man. He had planned to walk down the aisle of the church, as a father is supposed to do, as he is expected to do, accompanying April, who would wear a demure white dress and carry a white bouquet. Her present actions were unseemly and unconventional, as they always had been, even for modern times. Her name was fitting; she was flighty, capricious, and unpredictable.

He did not cut her out of his will, and even if he had, it wouldn't have made much difference. He erased her name from the family Bible so neatly and completely it was hard to tell that April was ever there.

When April and her young man decided to marry, he was even more disturbed, for he did not like to reverse the accepted order of things. For the wedding in a park, on a Saturday morning, April wore a too-short dress embroidered with red geraniums. Her mother cried and embraced them all.

April and her young man produced three boys and one girl. One of the boys was neat and methodical.

Eventually April's father died, but he had realized that death was in the plan. They dug his grave precisely, for they knew he would want it that way.

But April's children, the three noisy ones, scattered dozens of red roses, taken from the funeral flowers, over the cold wet earth in which he slept. Then they held hands, singing as they wept, and danced around his grave telling him good-bye.

And in the springtime and all future springtimes he was covered with rambling tangled bushes and masses of crimson flamboyant blossoms that dropped untidy petals.

REMEMBERING RUTH

Madge H. Lewis

My friend who was one with the land
Has now become part of that blessed earth she loved.
Health that cast a glow about her life
Departed.

Her voice that spoke as no other I have heard
Was stilled at first. Her eyes betrayed the thoughts inside.
Poetry and music, the beauty of mind and soul remained
Unthwarted.

She lived awhile, not whole again but almost so,
Adrift in the backwash of her sanity, clothed in fatigue,
Struggling back to us, in a strange and lonely sea
Uncharted.

We thought she would not leave us then,
We heard again the laughter and the music.
"Do you think the rocks and paths remember me?" she said,
Lighthearted.

Those things she always loved,
They must be with her in her special resting place,
Taken there on eagles' wings the day that we were
Parted.

In loving memory of Ruth Graves Russell
Member of the Memphis Story Tellers' League

THE FLIGHT HOME

Anne H. Norris

TRUDGING along toward Gate 36 with a bag of San Francisco sourdough bread in one hand, attaché case in the other, and raincoat over my arm, I wondered why my flight always seemed to depart from the farthest gate. I was in pain. My head ached. My feet ached. Parts in between felt like I had been hit by a runaway cable car.

San Francisco is a wonderful city, but a four-day convention there can do terrible things to one's body. I was ready for Memphis and a quiet weekend at home.

It is my policy never to fly on a Friday afternoon unless absolutely necessary. But this was a necessity. If I didn't make this flight it would mean a cab back to the hotel and another night away from my family. I could see a crowd milling around at the distant gate. I was sure the flight would be full, if not over-booked. I wouldn't volunteer to give up my seat if they offered a free round-trip ticket to Paris. All I wanted to do was board the plane, get settled into my reserved aisle seat, and sleep all the way home. I was considering faking a sprained ankle so I could get early boarding privilege with those needing assistance or a little extra time. However, by the time I finally reached the gate, boarding by rows had begun.

I eased into the long line and gave a sigh of relief that I was about to board. I tried to return the flight attendant's cheerful greeting, but my forced smile lasted only a minute. In my aisle seat was a grandmotherly–looking lady, buckled in and settled down for the flight. I suggested that she move over next to the window, explaining that she was in my seat.

"No," she said, "This is where they told me to sit."

She had no intention of moving, and I had no intention of taking the window seat. I like an aisle seat and this was the one I had reserved. I bucked the oncoming passengers to solicit help from the flight attendant, whose smile was beginning to fade.

It was with great reluctance that the old lady finally moved. The flight attendant had explained that she could now look out the window. That was not a good selling point. She did not want to look out. She was sure if she was looking out when we took off, she would get air sick. She wanted me to let her know when we were in the air. I promised I would.

I closed my eyes, hoping for peace and quiet. Not to be had. The little lady proceeded to inform me that she had gone to California on a bus to visit her son. Just a few days before she was to return home, she had twisted her ankle. The doctor had said she should keep it elevated as much as possible to prevent swelling. Realizing it now would not be advisable for her to spend several days on the bus, her son had purchased the plane ticket. This was the first time she had ever flown. This I believed to be true.

In my semi–conscious state, I later realized that we were still on the ground. I managed to focus my eyes on my faithful Timex and could see we should have been well on our way. The flight attendant soon was passing down the aisle, explaining our delay. Of course I had to repeat her message to the old lady beside me.

"One of the toilets is out of order," I said, "and since the plane is fully loaded and the flight will be several hours, they want to get it repaired before we take off."

She shrugged her shoulders and said, "Well, I wasn't planning to use the toilet before we get to Memphis anyway." I could see smiles on faces of passengers to the front, rear and side of us. The fun had only just begun!

Faithful to my promise, I informed the little lady when at last we were airborne.

"Are we going to have a movie now?" she asked.

"No, ma'am. Movies are shown only on the big planes," I said. I could see the disappointment on her face as she looked at me in total bewilderment.

"But isn't this a big plane?" she asked.

I reminded myself that this was her first flight. Moreover, I had been taught to respect my elders. I pointed out, with what patience I could muster, that the plane was small compared to the jumbo jets, and it did not have a screen on which movies could be shown.

I was saved from further discussion of in–flight movies with the arrival of the flight attendant, once again smiling as she pushed the drink cart. A cup of black coffee was just what I needed. The little lady was adamant that she wanted nothing.

"Maybe you would like a glass of juice," I suggested. Looking me right in the eye, she told me in no uncertain terms that she did not want juice or anything else. I smiled to myself, recalling that she had said she didn't plan to use the restroom until we got to Memphis. I figured she had decided against any liquid intake.

It was not until the passengers several rows ahead had been served that she turned to me and asked what would be the cost of a glass of orange juice. She looked at me in such a child-like manner that the wall I had tried to put between us began to crumble. I explained that beverages were complimentary and called to the flight attendant that my friend in the window seat would like some orange juice.

She fumbled with her seat belt and asked for my assistance in unbuckling it. I must have been mistaken about the restroom matter. But no, she didn't want to go anywhere. She just didn't want the seat belt fastened. I explained the airline policy that all passengers are asked to keep their seat belts fastened as a safety precaution in the event turbulent weather should be experienced. She looked at me and then at several passengers moving down the aisle toward the rear of the plane.

"Where are those people going?" she asked.

"Probably to the restroom," I replied, wondering why she couldn't figure that out herself.

"Well," she said very matter-of-factly, "I guess they must have their seat belts unfastened." I leaned over and released the buckle on her seat belt.

Choosing which entree she would have at mealtime was a big decision. Her son had explained to her that the meal was included in the price of the ticket even though he had failed to tell her about the complimentary beverages. Now she wanted my opinion. Should she have the baked chicken or the lasagna? She didn't want anything that might upset her stomach. I agreed with her on that! I suggested the chicken—for both of us.

Personally, I preferred lasagna. But I had a feeling if I got lasagna, she would decide my meal looked better than hers and would want me to summon the flight attendant and get her meal changed.

Chicken was a good choice. She had no complaints about the meal. The trays were removed. It was nap time. I had hardly closed my eyes before I felt her tugging at my sleeve. "Why are we flying along the highway?" she asked as she pointed out the window.

At 35,000 feet, above a layer of clouds, I knew there was no possible way she could be seeing the highway. At her insistence, I leaned over to look. I'm not sure that I ever really convinced her what she was seeing was the wing of our plane.

Finally she dozed off. No more than ten minutes later, she was awake and ready for more conversation. I was informed that she lived in Arkansas, but she had to fly to Memphis because that was the nearest airport. Her son had arranged for one of her neighbors to meet her when she arrived, and this nice man would drive her to her home in Marion, Arkansas.

I welcomed the announcement that we were in the approach pattern for the Memphis International Airport; albeit the flight certainly had not been boring. The flight attendant suddenly appeared, holding forth a bottle of champagne toward my seat companion. "For you," she said to the lady, "to celebrate your first plane ride."

My friend, as I now had come to consider her, looked to me for an explanation. "It's a bottle of champagne, a gift from the airline, so you will remember your first flight."

Her comment was emphatic. "I don't drink."

Now it was the flight attendant's turn to be baffled. She was not accustomed to anyone turning down a bottle of champagne. I suggested to my traveling companion that she reconsider. Surely she must know someone whom she could give it to. She reckoned her neighbor who was meeting her in Memphis would appreciate it. So it was settled. She accepted the gift, although rather reluctantly.

As soon as we had landed and the seat belt sign was turned off, she was standing, ready to deplane. Leaning impatiently on the back of the seat in front of her and looking over the shoulder of the gentleman still seated there, she declared loud enough to be heard by those in the rear of the plane, "This man just had his first flight, too."

I could feel eyes turning our way as I asked how she came by this information. "Because he's got a bottle of champagne too," she informed me, as well as all the other passengers within earshot.

This was too much. I peered over the seat to see that bottle of champagne for myself. The man whose ears now were turning from pink to red did not have a bottle of champagne. What he had was a folding umbrella, with the handle upturned.

The passengers had begun to move forward. I stepped into the aisle and made room ahead of me for the little lady, clutching her bottle of champagne. I knew why the other passengers were smiling. At least they had enjoyed in–flight entertainment.

The entire crew was lined up at the front of the plane. As I approached the door, one of the flight attendants reached out to present me with a bottle of champagne.

"This one is for you, with our appreciation. You deserve it."

Unlike the lady from Arkansas, I readily accepted the gift.

THE WINE LIST

Ethel Joyner

Which wine to serve for my dinner guests?
Which could pass the connoisseur's test?
Suddenly, I'm beyond a plebeian existence
And carried aloft to vineyards distant
Where I sample vintages, the exotic and rare,
And renounce the jug wine, the vin ordinaire.
I snap back to reality, a voice is speaking,
"Pardon me, madam, what wine are you seeking?"
"A full-bodied wine with a fragrant bouquet;
I'll have no ordinary wine bottled yesterday."
"We have a Chateau LaFite that would be nice."
With a tremulous voice, I inquired the price.
"One hundred dollars for this fine estate wine."
"Thank you so much. I'll be back another time."
I poured from the jug a hearty burgundy wine;
My guests were impressed and liked it just fine.

THE THIEF

Ann J. Huckaba

NOTHING could have been more disconcerting than coming to the realization that a thief was living in or had access to our house. Now, I don't mean someone was stealing the family silver or that my jewelry was missing piece by piece, but little things—a cashmere glove from my dressing table, a small fur toy I'd had for years, and other things like hair rollers, a nylon stocking and a full pack of pipe cleaners from my husband's work table.

Most disturbing of all was a situation that arose when a friend came to visit. At the end of her stay, she packed her bag but did not immediately close the lid and lock it. When she went to do so, she found the suitcase had been rifled, with clothes on the floor all around the luggage rack. A missing scarf was found on the closet floor, a hair net located under the chair, a belt near the bed. She just dismissed the hair rollers because she probably had not brought as many as she thought.

I was embarrassed and distressed, to say the least. I could not even suggest that there might be a ghost in the house. Neither of us would buy that story. Besides, what would a ghost do with pipe cleaners and hair rollers?

Was some neighborhood child slipping into the house and taking these things? The missing items were nothing a burglar would want. My friend's open pocketbook on a table had been disturbed, but no money taken. I was becoming very concerned over these events and had no explanation.

One afternoon shortly afterwards, I was busy sewing in an upstairs room when suddenly there were strange, thumping noises I could not identify. It was cause for alarm, in view of what had been taking place, and because the back kitchen door was open a bit to allow our beautiful Siamese kitty to come and go. He was not yet a year old and became upset when he could not immediately get into the house if he became frightened. He loved being outside, especially since becoming great friends with Big Jim, a huge, gray striper who lived directly back of us. They played tag, hide–and–seek, and chase–the–squirrel in our garden. Until these recent incidents we had never had a problem or an intruder, and felt comfortable leaving the door ajar.

As I left my sewing to investigate the noise, I admitted to some degree of apprehension. I visualized a burglar rummaging drawers, opening and closing cupboards, and overturning furniture. Very foolishly, instead of quietly leaving the house and calling the police, I walked down the hall to see what was going on.

The noise stopped abruptly, but not before I determined it came from the guest bedroom. Walking very softly then, I reached the door and looked all around. No one was there, but in scanning the room I spied one big, yellow eye—frozen still—peering at me from under the dust ruffle and behind a full-length table skirt by the bed.

I, too, froze.

For several seconds we looked eyeball to eyeball, with not a movement or sound from either of us. Maybe I was a bit slow, but I finally realized that enormous yellow eye had to belong to Big Jim, and no doubt there was a blue-eyed Siamese kitty under there with him, neither of them moving a muscle.

It was a great relief to know the cats were the source of the noise and not some petty thug in the house, or, at the least, some neighborhood child. I was curious to know what they would do next and to see if they thought I had discovered them. I turned and walked down the hall with deliberate steps, making it obvious I had left the room. Sure enough, they thought they had put one over on me and the beating and banging resumed and continued for some time, then ceased. Cats can move as quietly as a shadow, yet can sound like a herd of elephants when they so choose—and that's the way they went down the stairs and out the kitchen door into the garden.

Now to answer the question on my mind: what was the attraction under the bed? On hands and knees I lifted the bed skirt. What a revelation—and what a sight! There, scattered about under that bed, was a glove, a hair net, my fur toy, many pipe cleaners, several other missing items, and a very fine collection of hair rollers. Our beautiful Siamese kitty was a thief! Not only that, he had the audacity to bring his playmate in to show off his stash of goodies—and to spend an hour or so with them under that bed, behind those bed skirts, in their own little playhouse.

How could I have not suspected a real cat burglar? For one thing, that little beast was not only magnificent to look at, he was smart. Not once did he ever let us see him abscond with some attractive plunder. He had it accurately figured out he was not supposed to have those things and, therefore, carefully chose his time to move them to his hiding place.

I did not immediately remove the collection but left it for the cats to enjoy a while longer. They would come into the house, go directly up the stairs to that bedroom, play for a while, then leave. In a few days we decided it was time to keep the kitchen door closed and locked, and to clean out the guest room.

Thereafter, when anything in the house disappeared from its proper place, an immediate check under the bed would usually reveal its whereabouts and it could be retrieved—over the very vocal protestations of our Siamese that he was being robbed!

SATURDAY'S WOMAN

Madge H. Lewis

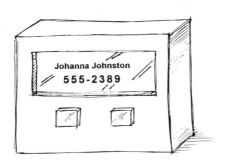

PENELOPE grabbed the phone on the second ring, glancing excitedly at her new Caller ID display. The device, only one hour old, flashed its first message for her:

Johanna Johnston, 555-2389, 5:30 pm,
Saturday, July 28

She didn't want to get into a long–winded conversation with her best friend right now in case Jeremy might call to say he'd be home early this once. Maybe she could cut the conversation short.

She was so lost in her thoughts that she didn't realize she hadn't said anything yet until she heard Jeremy's baritone. "Hi, Pen. Are you there?"

"Yes..." Jeremy? She stared at the display unit. But what was he doing at Johanna's house?

"I thought maybe Mandy had picked up the phone, it took you so long to say something. Are you okay?" He sounded concerned. She felt concerned herself—and confused. She waited a moment, thinking he'd explain why he was at Johanna's instead of at his office working on some architectural project he had used for six months as an excuse for his long hours away from home. When he said nothing she forced herself to answer, though her throat was so constricted the words sounded distorted.

"Sure. Fine. Mandy's taking a nap before tonight's cookout. I was just on my way to awaken her."

"I'm almost ready to leave the office." When Jeremy said those words Penelope felt a dizziness engulf her and she grabbed hold of the chair beside her. "So if you'll put the charcoal on the grill now it should be ready when I get there. I'll open a bottle of burgundy; it'll taste great with the hamburgers. Need anything picked up on the way?"

"No—no, I don't believe so." Penelope hung up abruptly. She couldn't trust herself to continue talking while she stared at the Caller ID, the purveyor of information that clarified vague suspicions she'd had for six months.

She sank into the nearest chair. She felt beyond tears. Her universe had suddenly narrowed into this shocking moment in time. Finally, when she could think, the vague uneasiness of the past was focused and she saw the whole picture. How could she have been so stupid? She had allowed herself to become "just a housewife," while her friends had followed careers that made them exciting and amusing.

She remembered the last party they had attended—the Symphony Ball—and how much attention Jeremy had paid to two of the women guests. One was her best friend, the artistic and beautiful Johanna; another was witty, sophisticated Deborah. Both were successful in their careers as she would have been if Jeremy had not urged her to give up her position as executive assistant to the owner of a large travel agency when she became pregnant with Mandy.

She had spent these years making their house a place where they belonged as a family, with a sense of unity that was fixed and solid, unmarred by the cares of the outside world. In those early years they'd lived with thrift store tables and hand-me-down chairs while Jeremy finished school. They'd been happy. She looked about the room remembering the dreams she and Jeremy had shared of completing the furnishing of their house. Now she no longer cared about the graceful wing chair and the elegant oil paintings they had admired. She was not the least interested in the exquisite early Biedermeier desk she had yearned for at Enderby's Antiques. Her home—her life—was complete only when they were together. Their Saturdays had always been important—happy times reserved for just the three of them.

She'd believed him at first when he told her he had a special project at his architectural firm and would have to work every Saturday. When the weeks dragged on and he made no mention of anticipating the end of the assignment she became suspicious. Could there be another woman—one who was glowing, stimulating and more than willing to fill his Saturdays with excitement? Now she knew—yet never would she have suspected it would be her beloved childhood friend Johanna.

Penelope determined there would be no tears, no recriminations. She had too much pride.

When she was as composed as she could ever be again, she went into Mandy's bedroom to awaken her from her nap. "Daddy's on his way home, darling. Do you want to get up and dressed for our Saturday night cookout?"

Mandy's rosy face just awakened from sleep, was lighted by her drowsy smile that displayed her sparkling baby teeth. Her tousled golden hair fanned out on the pillow. She threw her arms around Penelope's neck, her kiss brushing her cheek like the flutter of fairy wings.

"I'm glad Daddy will be home soon tonight." And when there was no answer, Mandy turned her questioning blue eyes toward her mother. "Aren't you, Mommy?"

Penelope nodded, not trusting herself to speak, as Mandy chattered gleefully while dressing. They went to the patio to start the coals in the grill. Afterwards Mandy chased butterflies and Penelope sat on the chaise longue and stared into the flame.

When she heard the car enter the driveway, Mandy ran to the iron grillwork gate. Mandy loved to play her special game with Daddy when he came home. Penelope watched them with mixed emotions, her tall, handsome, two–timing husband and their adorable daughter. His dark hair and intelligent brown eyes contrasted sharply with Mandy's golden beauty.

Jeremy regarded his daughter seriously and said, "Hello. Are you the lady of the house?"

"Yes, I am," Mandy replied in a grown-up tone of voice. "What can I do for you, sir?"

"Well," Jeremy said and Penelope saw that he was repressing a smile, "I have a fine product here and I would like to come in and show it to you."

"I'm sorry, sir. My Daddy told me never to talk to strangers, so I 'spose you can't come in."

"But this will take only a moment of your valuable time, Madame." Jeremy slowly moved his right arm from behind and brought forth the latest Barbie Doll.

Mandy's eyes opened wide. Penelope knew she'd been dying for this particular Barbie Doll, but she was apparently having too much fun with Daddy to quit now.

"No, I can't let you in," Mandy said, looking back at Penelope with her hand over her mouth, trying hard to restrain a conspiratorial chuckle. "I guess you'll have to go to another house."

"That's too bad," Jeremy said, turning away.

"Daddy, Daddy," she cried out, "don't go away. You can come in." And she opened the gate, hugging him around the knees as soon as he entered.

He placed the doll for Mandy on a nearby table and lifted her high into the air as she squealed and giggled. Then he turned toward Penelope, but she quickly got up, without a greeting and walked toward the grill.

"I'll get the wine," he said as he strode into the house, seemingly unaware of her stony silence, "and some lemonade for Mandy."

Why couldn't this be like earlier Saturday evenings, a time to treasure? Penelope felt the tears well up in her eyes, but hastily got control of herself. She didn't want Mandy to see that she was sad, but more than that, she would never let Jeremy sense how vulnerable she was.

He returned with the wine and glasses on a tray, balanced on one hand like a waiter for Mandy's amusement, and then handed her an icy lemonade in her special plastic glass.

"Thank you, Daddy," Mandy said as she held up her Barbie Doll. "I'm going to be very careful so Barbie won't get any of my lemonade on her dress."

The hamburgers were sizzling on the grill and the aroma filled the air. Jeremy turned on the sound system he had put together so they would have background music when they sat on the patio. It had always been a source of pleasure to them when they had their Saturday night cookouts.

"Why so quiet, Pen?" Jeremy asked as he filled her glass. "Did you have a bad day?"

"No," she answered quietly, not allowing herself to broach the subject that was breaking her heart. "Just thinking."

The evening seemed interminable to Penelope, and she wondered how Jeremy and Mandy could seem so happy when she was so miserable. The food tasted like sawdust and she almost choked on the wine. Finally, she could no longer stand the tension and got up, flinging back the words, "I'm going in now. You two can stay out here if you like."

"We'll go in, too," Jeremy hoisted Mandy up onto his back and they followed her to the door that Penelope had intended to slam. But they trooped into the kitchen right behind her, Mandy chattering all the way and Jeremy humming a tune to the music.

A kitchen chair stood in the hallway leading to the great room. "Did you move that?" she asked.

"No."

"Well, if you didn't..." She felt her skin prickle. Had someone been in their house?

She rushed to the great room with Jeremy and Mandy right on her heels. When she got inside the doorway she stopped so abruptly that the three of them almost fell in a heap on the floor. Then Jeremy steadied his two girls and said quietly, "Pen, look over the mantel. Your birthday is next week, and I've been working on your gift for six months. I had Dan, Johanna's latest friend, hang it while we were outside. That's why I turned on the music so loud, hoping you wouldn't hear the noise."

Penelope's pent–up tears flowed. Above the mantel hung an oil painting—she recognized it as a color rendition of a black and white photograph Jeremy had taken of her on the day he had proposed.

They had been on a picnic, and he had captured in oils the symmetry of the setting, in the pale coral of her gauzy dress, her blonde hair that blew in the breeze, the horizon blue and blurred. Her feet were bare in the green grass and a daisy chain draped her head like a tiara while she held a bunch of daffodils in the crook of her arm. He had captured the essence of her, her great capacity for love, her dreamlike quality.

"Mommy, it's you!" Mandy said, clapping her hands together as she gazed upward at the portrait.

Jeremy put his arm around Penelope. "My architect duties taught me the basics, but your wonderful friend, Johanna, gave me private oil painting lessons for the last six months. She's more thrilled over it than you can imagine. Hope you like it, darling."

Penelope turned to him and the tears on her cheeks told him the answer. It was beautiful. But, most important of all, she felt Jeremy was home again—and she knew he'd never really left.

MILLICENT AND ME

Faye Livingston

ONCE upon a memory—and what a joy this memory is—I shared a friendship with a special lady named Millicent. I consider it my treasured destiny to have known her and hope to bring her to life for you by telling you about her and her talent as a poet.

Lyrical lines seemed to flow easily from her in conversation, as well as when she was alone with pen in hand, in the second story of her home in what she called her "Sky Parlor." Who was this lady in the Sky Parlor? Let me tell you who she really was.

It all began in Red Cloud, Nebraska, where she and Willa Cather, the famous poet, novelist, and journalist spent their childhood years. This relationship was one of Millicent's most treasured memories. They shared a deep love for Nebraska's prairies as well as the native trees, the cottonwoods, the poplars, the groves of ash and elms that were dear to the hearts of the pioneers. She cherished this bond through Willa Cather's life, through her school years, and her writing years. Millicent rejoiced when her childhood friend received praise in 1921 from Sinclair Lewis who proclaimed that "through her stories she has made the outside world know Nebraska as no one else has done." Two years later Willa Cather was awarded the Pulitzer Prize for her novel *One of Ours*.

Millicent did not equate her own talents with those of her famous friend. Her own forte was verse. She did venture a few short stories, mostly for children, but poetry was her haven, her life. She truly mourned when Willa Cather died, and her own writing at that time reflected how keenly she felt the loss of this literary friend.

When Millicent's parents died in an influenza epidemic, she was sent to her sister in McCook, Nebraska. There she lived in a home of loving and caring and later wrote this poignant passage: *"I would rather not have lived than to have missed being the sister of such a woman as my sister-mother."*

Millicent attended Normal College in Peru, Nebraska where, after two years, she was awarded her teaching certificate. How proud she was of that schooling in the early 1900s, as it was rare for women of those times to have such an education. She was also delighted that the graduation address was given by the author and philosopher Elbert Hubbard. A friendship developed from this encounter; later she made a visit to Mr. Hubbard's home in New York and had afternoon tea with him—another daring adventure for a woman of that era.

Following her award of a teaching certificate, she returned to McCook and began her career as a kindergarten teacher. Oh! she did love those children, and she formed lasting relationships with many of her pupils. One of those students introduced us to each other and thus began my friendship with Millicent. We realized immediately that we were kindred spirits.

After spending the first years of her career as a teacher, it was a natural step for her to become a librarian. The children of the town looked to her for help, as she described in this poem about an errant Tom Sawyer type who came to her for assistance.

> *Hey—Miss Millicent!*
> *I gotta make a book report*
> *So gimme a book that's very short*
> *A book with lots of good big print*
> *With quite a lot of pictures in't,*
> *With margins wide and pages stout--*
> *I don't care much what it's about.*
> *But I am in an awful stew*
> *As this report's now overdue*
> *My teacher just gave me the warning*
> *It must be in tomorrow morning!"*

Millicent called the Andrew Carnegie structure on Main Street, in which the library was housed, her "Spanish Villa on the Hill." Neighbors on that same street were US Senator and Mrs. George William Norris. Senator Norris was author of the bill to create the Tennessee Valley Authority, and a dam on the Tennessee was named in his honor. Millicent and Mrs. Norris were dear and longtime friends.

Millicent knew how to milk all the good things from life. Her work, her chosen friends, all of her daily activities—when it came to "milking" things, she was an expert dairy maid!

Perhaps the best way to really get to know Millicent is to hear about what she called her "Scribble Books." In these she wrote her beautiful, poetic thoughts and her observations about the interesting life that surrounded her. I don't know how many of these literary gems are floating around—four or five, maybe more. I have two of them, so let me share a few bits and pieces with you. This poem was published in *Ideals* Magazine:

> *The heart of a child*
> *Is a tremulous thing;*
> *Lovely and frail*
> *As a butterfly's wing*
> *Kissed by the beam*
> *Of a summer sun,*
> *Or crushed by the word*
> *Of a careless one.*
> *A look or a smile*
> *Will cause it to sing*
> *For the heart of a child*
> *Is a tremulous thing.*

I guess the warmest remembrances would be of visits to her Sky Parlor. She lived just across the street and down a little from the library. Most of us who knew her have been privileged with a warm encounter there, a cup of tea, the pearls of verse and wisdom she could so easily come up with. She would reach out from her antique rocker for a book to show the passage that lurked in her memory, sharing her contagious enthusiasm with the listener. To complete her cozy corner was her grandmother's spinning wheel. And, how she loved having folks drop in! This is what she wrote about visitors...

> *"Guest, you are welcome,*
> *Be at your ease.*
> *Get up when you're ready*
> *Go to bed when you please.*
> *Happy to share with you*
> *Such as we've got*
> *The leak in the roof*

And the soup in the pot.
You don't have to thank us
Or laugh at our jokes.
Sit deep and come often
You're one of the folks. "

If you perchance supped on her porch overlooking the garden area, especially in spring you would have heard this verse:

"I used to love my garden
But now my love is dead
For I found a Bachelor Button
In Black Eyed Susan's bed!"

Millicent's life was filled with poetry. Even with these visible keepsakes we have of her, we who knew her are inclined to feel that her true treasures were within her person. Her convictions, her warmth, her giving. With Millicent it was not just what was needed–it was above and beyond the call. She lived to be 101 years old and lost all her contemporary friends in the last part of her life and many more who were twenty and thirty years younger. It was difficult for her to experience the loss of so many of those she loved.

One day as life style changes caused her to come face to face with her own mortality, she gave me her thirteen-volume set of Elbert Hubbard's works, saying she wanted me to have them. She knew I would treasure them as she did. I assured her that the gifts from her need not be material, but rather the parts of our lives that we shared through prose and poetry. Her eyes sparkled with unshed tears of enthusiasm that day as she related her many tales of the special friendships she had enjoyed during her life. This is what she wrote in memory of those who had gone before her:

"This morning when the sun came up
And filled my lonely room
It seemed to bring a friendly smile
To overcome my gloom.
I could inhale the fragrance
Of the flowers everywhere
And taste the steaming coffee
That we always used to share.
And I could almost hear your voice
And the look of your soft eyes
With never any argument
Or the need to compromise.
But when the sun reached up beyond
The hour that was dawn,
I remembered deep within my heart–
You were not here, but gone."

Her letters to Memphis tugged at my heart because of her longing for visits from me. She yearned for times together, to live again amid the memories of our beloved prose and poetry.

When a visit was finally possible she expressed her enjoyment at my being there and asked, "When will you be coming again?" In reply I wrote a poem for her that personified the living, loving person she was. It is titled...

Daydreams

"Once a day and sometimes more
You knock upon my daydream door
And I say warmly, "Come right in.
I'm glad you're here with me again."
Then we'd sit down and have a chat,
Recalling this - discussing that,
Until some task that I must do
Forces me away from you.

Reluctantly I say good-bye,
Smiling with a little sigh,
For though my daydreams bring you near
I wish that you were really here.

But what reality can't change
My daydream wishes can arrange
And through my wishing you'll be brought
To me each day -- a guest in thought."

Finally that inevitable day came when we ourselves had to say farewell to Millicent, to put her to rest beneath the summer sky, to bless the land that was to receive her heart amid the yellow wheat and the rustling corn of our beloved Nebraska.

HERALD OF SPRING

Anne H. Norris

Winter's cold is almost gone,
    A friend told me today;
He stopped to spread the tidings
    That spring is on the way.

Quite a sassy one was he,
    In his sleek red vest;
To sing of spring's arrival,
    He really looked his best.

I saw him turn a time or two;
    He whistled a happy tune,
As if to say his many friends
    Would be arriving soon.

Sporty little friend of mine,
    What a joy you bring.
In my heart I sing with you,
    O Robin, herald of spring.

THE AWARD

Ethel Joyner

CALVIN believed until the day he died that someday the ten-million dollar Publisher's Clearing House Award would be his. He fantasized over the day that he would open the door to the beaming face of the bearer of the good news while the cameras captured the expression of joy on his face at that unforgettable moment. He could see the headlines in the daily paper heralding the news: "Calvin Jones Wins 10-Million Dollar Award." He would be inundated with congratulatory messages from former co–workers, friends and relatives, all of whom would be secretly envious of his newly–acquired wealth.

The hours weighed heavily on Calvin during his retirement years, and many a day was spent in reflecting how quickly the years had sped by, and how time was rapidly becoming his adversary in the fulfillment of his life-long dream. He went back over the forty–five years he had shared with Agnes. She had accepted the responsibilities of juggling the household budget and of making the most of Calvin's earnings to rear and educate their two children, certainly with no frills, but through her careful, frugal management, they had maintained a decent lifestyle.

Agnes accepted with quiet resignation the knowledge that Calvin would never be a great achiever when he was passed over time after time for promotions, advancing very little in his job.

Calvin never felt bitter or resentful that success in the work place had eluded him; he was seemingly indifferent. Always the eternal optimist, he believed that great things lay in store for him. He loved to daydream of the time when he and Agnes would embark on a world cruise in a luxury suite on the QE2. He rationalized that though Agnes's rewards would come late in life, they would nonetheless be sweet and satisfying—new cars, new house, and with it the respect and prestige of an affluent lifestyle.

The Publisher's Clearing House regularly sent Calvin opportunities to win the award. They made it clear that one was not obligated to subscribe to their publications to be a winner, but it was implied that it would certainly enhance one's opportunities. Calvin would dutifully make his choices from a selection sheet, mailing it along with his check to the publisher's address where his name was added to a giant reservoir containing countless names of like-minded, would-be millionaires.

At first, Calvin used restraint, ordering a few of his favorite magazines, but he could not resist the "You Too Can Be A Millionaire" letters sent by the publisher and began to respond to them with increased frequency.

Agnes began to dread the postman's visits. In turn, the postman, muttering audible oaths, was becoming more hostile as he delivered to the Jones's burgeoning mailbox the daily avalanche of magazines. Agnes and the mailman were Calvin's victims as he blithely continued his pursuit of the award.

Early on, Agnes tried to read the magazines, but it became a hopeless task; they overwhelmed her. In addition to conventional magazines on sports, travel, cuisine, mechanics, home decorating and tabloids, the daily delivery brought instructive manuals on how to build most anything, from vacation homes and additions, to garages and storm cellars.

What to do with the magazines became a matter of mounting concern. She wracked her brain for a solution, finally devising a system in which she stacked them by category in her guest bedroom. Once her pride and joy, a tribute to her decorating skills, the guest room became a repository for the magazines, the stacks reaching ever higher for the ceiling. She experienced moments of panic as she visualized the two of them found drowned in a sea of newsprint, reminiscent of the paper–congested house in which the famed Collier brothers were discovered.

As her level of anxiety rose, her pleadings with Calvin grew more frequent and shrill. Calvin knew how to tune her out, and did so with regularity, all the while making promises to discontinue the subscriptions, although when old ones ran out, new ones would appear.

Agnes's growing resentment could no longer be contained, and she sought counseling in a desperate attempt to find a resolution to her dilemma. Her therapist encouraged her to speak freely and openly of the problems that had beset her in her marriage to Calvin. Uncovering stifled resentments, she recalled that her mother–in–law, like Calvin, believed until her ninety–seventh year (the year in which she died) that instant wealth was just around the corner. She believed that she was an heir to valuable real estate on Manhattan Island through a long-standing tale of doubtful origin that had been passed down for generations in her family. Calvin had inherited from his mother a genetic predisposition to live in a fantasy world.

The therapist, in an effort to help Agnes gain insight into the reasons for Calvin's irrational behavior, explained his conclusions: Calvin had in place a protective shield that permitted him to ward off dealing with reality. He coped with his failures and inadequacies by escaping to a make–believe world where the acquisition of great wealth would gain him the esteem that had eluded him throughout his life.

An enlightened Agnes began to better understand her husband through the intensive counseling sessions. The nagging ceased, even though the stacks of magazines continued to build. Quiet resentment persisted as she made her daily treks to the overflowing mailbox, sometimes encountering the exasperated mailman struggling with the weight of the bag on his back.

A few years into his retirement, Calvin became ill and was an invalid confined to the house, but hope remained in his heart for the knock on the door. Even as his health declined, he faithfully continued to send the publisher his magazine selections.

Agnes went through a grieving process after Calvin's death, and for a few months she forgot about her problem. But then with the realization that she need no longer be swamped with magazines, she experienced a sense of freedom and exhilaration as she began to cancel the subscriptions. She decided to contribute the magazines to charitable institutions, and little by little the stacks diminished until finally there were none. Agnes reclaimed her guest bedroom.

The contents of the mailbox lessened until it contained only routine mail, except for the day she noted an unstamped envelope in the box bearing her name. Opening it, she read: "Dear Mrs. Jones, I wish to extend to you condolences on the death of your husband. I must say, however, my chiropractor has noted a miraculous improvement in the condition of my back and has dismissed me from further treatment." It was signed: "Gratefully, your mailman."

DEATH AND THE CLEANING WOMAN

Malra Treece

MRS. O'CALLAHAN'S bunions hurt, and the pail of mop water seemed heavier than in the twenty–four years she had been cleaning the English building. Her back hurt, too. Sometime soon she would probably kick the bucket.

She knew that Professor Knox, the literature professor whose classroom she was cleaning, would consider "kick the bucket" a euphemism. (It had taken her forever to find the word in the dictionary after he had used it in class). Now she knew that euphemism is a trite, meaningless phrase for die, but surely kicking the bucket must be more fun than dying.

Immediately she did kick the bucket. She slipped in a puddle of water she had spilled and kicked over the bucket and slammed her head against the edge of a student desk.

She knew at once that she was dead. No more mops or dusting books, no more teachers' dirty looks.

She wondered why she wasn't in Heaven. She had lived respectably enough, goodness knows. Dully, but respectably. It might take a little while. Saint Peter probably didn't know about it yet or he would have sent a carriage for her.

Suddenly she was above the campus, sailing over the top of the red and gold maples. She stopped to rest on a low white cloud.

The campus looked so beautiful that she hated to leave it. Once more she wanted to walk the winding pathways and look at the young folks. Now that she was dead they wouldn't expect her to dust. She would sit in the library and read the books of poetry that Professor Knox talked about. She had bought Emily Dickinson's poems, in a big book that cost almost a day's pay, but there are many other poets. She would read them all.

She would watch the moon rise over the river and feel the rain in her hair and eat grapes and sleep until noon. But just once more she wanted to sit in the storage closet next to the classroom, where she always ate her lunch, and listen to Professor Knox teach the literature class. Maybe now that she was dead she could understand him better. The Bible says that when we're alive we see through a glass darkly; the glass would be clearer now.

Too, she must feed the mouse that came each day to share her lunch. She had named the mouse Emily Dickinson, and she wondered if Emily would starve now. It occurred to her that the mouse was the only creature on Earth who really needed her, unless she counted the students and teachers for whom she cleaned. Nobody was in Heaven, either, that she was dying to see. She giggled at the word dying and wished there was somebody she could repeat it to.

She lay back on the billowy cloud. It was soft and enveloping, like a feather bed. She arranged the white puffs, made a large pillow, and buried her head in it. "I've got my head in the clouds today," she said aloud. "O'Callahan, old girl, you're getting right clever now that there's nobody to hear you."

Bits of cloud clung to her dress. She tried to brush them away. A body—that is, a person—ought to be able to stay neat long enough to get to Heaven.

A long white limousine appeared before her, driven by a man who looked too young to be Saint Peter or Death. He looked like a hippie.

"I thought you'd come in a carriage," she said. Emily Dickinson had written: *Because I could not stop for Death, he kindly stopped for me; The carriage held but just ourselves, and Immortality.*

The young man laughed. "Oh, we haven't used carriages for years, or so I'm told."

"Who are you?" she asked.

"I'm a chauffeur, GS-3. Civil Service, you know."

"I have decided not to go," she said.

"You jest, of course. Everybody goes."

"But I haven't finished the dusting, and there's nobody to feed Emily Dickinson, and—"

"There's no provision in the regulations to allow you to finish your work. When we come for you, you go. It's written in the code book, Volume 20, page 1997."

"Just give me a little time. Can't I just go back and wander the Earth a bit? I've spent most of my life cleaning the English Building."

Something like sympathy came into the boy's lean face. She wondered if he had also fallen on a mop bucket.

He answered without being asked. "No, I got mine in a street fight. I wasn't ready to go, either."

"I am going to wait for a carriage, like Emily Dickinson."

"You get into this big long white car—right now—or I'm going to tell Saint Peter. You're a lot luckier than some folks. You must have clout. I drive an old model pickup to get most people."

"Not now, please. You could spend more time on Earth, too, while you wait to take me."

He considered, then shook his head. "I'm still on probation."

"Not even a day? Tell your supervisor you had trouble with the car."

She wondered what had come over her. Not once that she could remember had she told a lie, not in her whole life.

The young man looked toward the Earth. "It is lovely."

"Just a little while," she pleaded. "Just one more day."

"It's a deal," he said. "Only a day, though. You'll meet me here at this same time tomorrow."

She was back in the classroom. The overturned bucket was still on the floor. Although the room was empty, she saw in her mind all the young faces that had occupied it, semester after semester, during the past twenty-four years. It was time for class. She heard laughing students coming up the stairs. Then they were crowding around her. They like me, she thought. They really like me. There was concern on their faces.

"It's all right," she said. "I've had a full life."

"Call the doctor," Professor Knox told one of the young men. "She has a nasty cut on her head. She hit it against something."

She rose unsteadily. Her head pounded and there was a crick in her back. Her bunions still hurt, but they would always hurt, and the streets of gold would probably be no softer than the concrete floors of the English Building.

"Sit down and rest," Professor Knox said. He seated her in his chair.

"The class will come to order," she said. She cleared her throat. She had often wished she was a professor, but now she could think of nothing to say. She cleared her throat again and looked out the window. She had seen professors do that. But she must speak. The class would not meet again before she was gone, and there was so much that they should know. Things she should have known when she was their age. And she would ask them to feed Emily Dickinson, the pregnant mouse in the closet. She must think of the words.

She frowned in concentration and opened her mouth.

"There's so much to say and do, and so little time."

"Time for what, Mrs. O'Callahan?" the professor asked.

"Time to live."

One of the young ladies giggled.

"There's a mouse in that closet," Mrs. O'Callahan said. "Her name is Emily Dickinson, and every day at noon, during this class, I'm in there listening to you, Professor Knox. You do a real fine job with American literature."

One of the boys walked to the closet. "The mouse is here all right," he said. "It even looks like Emily, only somewhat smaller."

75

The girl who had giggled giggled again.

"I won't be back," Mrs. O'Callahan said. "Goodbye. Thank you for letting me help you a little." She stepped down from the chair. Her feet were steady now. "I'll get to the cleaning. I must do an extra good job today."

"But your head—" a young girl exclaimed.

"I'll wash off the blood and it will be all right. Tell the doctor there is nothing he can do."

A sweet-faced girl on the front row reached forward and brushed something from Mrs. O'Callahan's dress. "You have dust all over you," she said. "Even in your hair."

Mrs. O'Callahan looked at the white particles that covered her dress and the many that had fallen to the floor. "That isn't dust," she said. "Those are bits of a cloud."

"Of course," Professor Knox said.

THE RESCUE

Ann J. Huckaba

THE WHITE half–grown kitten that appeared in my yard was no ordinary cat; in fact, he was an extraordinary cat, but that realization came to me somewhat later and in stages.

The fall weather was bringing cold temperatures and I felt sorry for this bit of white fur with the enormous, golden–yellow eyes. I wondered which neighbor belonged to him, and why he was not being fed. He was hungry but evidently had been well cared for up to that time. He was snow–white, clean, well filled out and apparently in good condition. Where was his home and why didn't he go there? I did not want this cat. There was no success in locating his owner, but I had no intention of taking him in and every day I explained that to him.

Of course I fed him and within a week he was taking his meals in my kitchen. After eating, he would look at me and immediately go out the door, which was left ajar.

I have learned never to underestimate the intuition and sensitivity of a cat. We had just lost a much–loved Siamese and were not at all ready to accept another pet. But persistence and patience brought about the inevitable. One morning this very affectionate kitty finished his breakfast and, instead of leaving as was his routine, sat down in the kitchen and looked at me with those big eyes. His communication was as clear as if he had spoken in people language. "I've learned to like it here, and I am not leaving again." One would have thought the adoption papers were drawn up and signed.

Well, what could I say? I picked him up and stroked his back—to which he always responded by putting his front paws and legs around my neck and rubbing his face along my cheek and jaw. He then made a thorough inspection of the house, going into every nook and cranny. Finally he settled into the best chair in the living room and there he remained asleep the entire day. He was home.

The reluctance we had in accepting that cat was almost immediately dismissed. That night he slept in a chair in our bedroom. The next morning my husband picked him up and told him he looked just like a little angel and we were going to call him "Angelo." And so we did.

During the years we lived with Angelo, we learned he was quite the neighborhood clown. There were many antics but the one that brought the most smiles was his habit of getting to the rooftop of our garage, or one of the neighboring houses, and lying on his stomach along the gable, his front legs extended forward with his paws crossed. There, like the Sphinx, he silently surveyed the passing traffic and the neighborhood activities until he became bored, or until he was satisfied all was well and he could come down.

One day a kitten came home with Angelo—the truth might be that Angelo brought him to us—a wild, dirty, hungry little beast that would develop into a beautiful long–haired, multi–colored cat, with a tail carried as elegantly as a plume on the hat of a Victorian lady. He never became very tame, but the adoration and affection he had for Angelo was amazing, and he followed him everywhere. I think Angelo liked him well enough, but his was more of a tolerant affection. He did not object to my feeding the kitten and eventually when Little Buddy (as we named him) got up enough courage to come into the kitchen to eat, Angelo accepted that also, even though cats are territorial and want no trespassers in their private places, however much fun they may be to play with.

Late one afternoon several weeks later, I was in the kitchen when a movement outside the window caught my eye. Angelo was climbing to the top of a fence post that allowed him to jump across a brick walkway to the garage roof. Little Buddy, who was much bigger now, watched as Angelo got all set and made the leap. Little Buddy's frustration was obvious; how on earth could he follow? Finally he climbed the post and there he stood, four feet bunched together, wondering what to do next. At last his desire to follow overpowered his fear and he, too, made the jump. He landed on the roof—but just barely. Never had I seen such pride; he strutted about shamelessly, that plume of a tail waving high.

Later when it was time for their supper, both cats were still on the roof. I called to them and immediately Angelo went to the roof's edge, carefully gauged the distance, and made a successful four-point landing on top of the post. He came into the kitchen and had started to eat when he heard the wailing of Little Buddy, still on the rooftop.

Angelo left his food, went to the door and looked out. What happened next I believe because I saw it. He went down the walk to the garage and stood there meowing, looking up at his stranded playmate. Little Buddy looked down at Angelo, then at the post. With the evident encouragement of Angelo's continued meowing, at last he made up his mind to do what it seemed he had to do, and high in the air he sailed across that walkway to the fence. His aim was fairly good and there was a great deal of clawing and scrambling, but he hung onto the top of that post, righted himself, then climbed down to the walk.

Angelo turned, marched back into the kitchen to finish his supper, followed by a very proud and grown–up Little Buddy. As Angelo came through the door, he glanced up at me with a look that clearly said, "These children."

THE TABLE

Madge H. Lewis

REMEMBERING the carefree days of early youth is like gathering wildflowers, a thought here, an image there, until there is a fragrant bouquet, a host of memories.

I can recall the moment of my inception and everything that has happened throughout the many years I have been in service. I was shaped and honed, lovingly carved and waxed by artistic hands—for I am a dining room table. From my polished surface, the great and the near–great have been served.

I think of myself as Mrs. Hamilton's table. She, it was, who gave the order to make me into an oval shape with a six inch apron. She specified a Queen Anne style with cabriole legs—and five leaves so that I could be expanded for the lavish parties she planned. Oh, what a masterpiece I was when I was placed in her elegant dining room, with the gas chandelier hanging precisely over the middle of my shining top!

The Table

The Hamiltons lived a comfortable patrician life in north Mississippi. The house was staffed with efficient servants and there were always sounds of quick busy feet before the dinner hour. I could tell from the weight of the big silver tureens and platters that they served bountiful meals. It was a magic time in the south—the Old South, it later was called.

Mrs. Hamilton allowed the children to eat in the dining room on special occasions, such as birthdays, Thanksgiving and Christmas. Young Timothy tried his very best to behave but it was foreign to his nature and I can remember Mr. Hamilton's scolding him and saying, "Timothy, if you do not sit still you will not be allowed to join us the next time." Timmy would be quiet, but not for long, and many times he was sent to his room, holding back his tears, for he was a manly lad.

Janie was a perfect young lady—or so her father thought. Unseen by Mr. Hamilton, she had a bad habit of kicking my beautifully carved legs. No one ever caught her but I have the scars today to prove it.

When the Civil War took Timmy away from us at the age of seventeen to fight the Yankees, life in the Hamilton house changed. War naturally took its toll on its easy graciousness. The laughter and the happy conversations of earlier years were gone; so were the lavish meals and the loving care of the household possessions. Most of the silver and china had been buried in the old rose garden.

I heard Mrs. Hamilton sob one day as she pleaded with her husband not to join the Confederate forces. "You don't have to go. Isn't it enough that Timmy is fighting for our cause? I can't bear it if you leave, too."

But Mr. Hamilton left, and his wife and Janie laid their heads on my dusty top and cried as though their hearts would break.

Memphis fell to the Yankees in 1862. Ulysses S. Grant stayed there for a short time, and after his military plans were completed, he proceeded with his troops to North Mississippi. He searched out the most comfortable accommodations. Unfortunately, our abode proved to his liking and, along with his troops, he moved into the Hamilton House. He banished to the attics Mrs. Hamilton and Janie and the two elderly servants who had remained behind. I heard him review his plans for the Vicksburg campaign with Major General W. T. Sherman and eight of his men as they sat around my perimeter, their heavy boots caked with mud, the air filled with the smoke of their cheap tobacco. They put their whiskey glasses down without any thought of protecting the precious solid walnut surface.

The master plan to take Vicksburg had been drawn up during Grant's stay in Memphis. Upon his arrival in Mississippi he had summoned Sherman to confer with him at Hamilton House. They went over the battle plans and I heard the details, noting with dread their certainty of a quick victory.

"We'll have control of the Mississippi River when Vicksburg falls!" General Grant bragged. After slamming his glass down on my surface, as though he had already accomplished his dastardly act, he took out his knife and began to carve his initials and the year onto my surface. They are still there today—*USG 1862*.

The following year, during the 47 day siege of Vicksburg, Mr. Hamilton died and in the midst of the family's grief, their house was converted to a hospital. I was used as an operating table, as many of the victims of Sherman's battles were brought here, and all the rooms were put to use.

When Timmy came home, he was minus his left leg. Mrs. Hamilton cried and cried and couldn't quit hugging him. Janie put her arms around both of them and the three Hamiltons stood there, not speaking, just letting their tears course down their cheeks. The war to preserve the American Union was over.

Timothy Hamilton married Elizabeth Purcell five years after he returned home and I was put into service for the occasion. The reception was not as lavish as in the old days, but everyone understood. People struggled through those times, but as the years passed, life gradually returned to normal. Timothy's children ate in the dining room on special days and I often heard him say to his oldest son, "Timmy, if you do not behave, I'll have to send you to your room." Many times, Timmy, Jr. would take his punishment like a man and depart in disgrace to his upstairs bedroom. Janie and her husband and children often came to visit and I was grateful that she was regularly seated toward the middle. I was still afraid of her kicks.

Three more Timothy Hamiltons lived at Hamilton House. The last one remained a bachelor and he often entertained his host of nieces and nephews. The meals were served elegantly. My fine surface was polished to a high gloss, but those hated initials still remained.

Other wars have taken place since the Civil War, but none have touched the Hamiltons so poignantly and so viciously. The house deteriorated after the last Timothy Hamilton died. It stood vacant for several years, but incredibly remained intact.

I was lonely during those years without my family. Sometimes I thought I could hear Mrs. Hamilton exclaim over a floral centerpiece placed properly under the chandelier. In my dreams I could feel her run her fingers softly over the beveled edge of my surface at the end where she always sat. I could almost hear her whisper in her soft, husky voice, "My table, my very special table."

Now, because memories linger in every corner, and because of its colorful history, Hamilton House is being refurbished by one of Janie's great–great–great grandsons and his wife, and will be completed in March. They will again sit around my gleaming top, the meals will be elegantly served, their children will be chastised if they misbehave. The gardens will come to life—the forsythia and daffodils will be a blaze of gold, followed by azaleas and dogwood, and red and yellow tulips pushing up through the pale blue forget–me–nots.

I shall listen to the comments; I shall treasure the compliments that are certain to be made about me—the gleaming, solid walnut, oval Queen Anne table with heavily carved cabriole legs. But deep inside I'll be thinking—you should have heard the things I have heard, felt the tears drop upon your surface, listened to the stories, watched those boys and girls grow up who lived exciting but sometimes tragic lives.

After the joys and sorrows the house has known, it will vibrate once again with the sound of busy feet, the lilting voices of children, life and laughter and southern hospitality—when spring comes.

THE FAMILY TREE CHALLENGE

Ethel Joyner

The children intrigued with the family tree,
Set out to learn more of their ancestry.
They pored over records in remote places,
Peered through albums of unfamiliar faces.
What they discovered as you will see
Eased not their crisis of identity.
Relatives unknown, ordinary, prosaic,
Were woven into the vast family mosaic.
Some, no doubt, were best left undiscovered,
As closeted skeletons were rapidly uncovered.
One entrepreneur operated a still by night.
Another, a scofflaw, had long taken flight.
One by a jealous husband had been shot.
One a wife beater, scoundrel, and sot.
It was revealed to be a motley crew,
Best described as a genealogical zoo.
The family tree challenge began to sour
On finding no one came over on the Mayflower.
Of all the relatives scattered far and wide,
Only one could be pointed to with family pride.
The relative, an eccentric, somewhat moronic,
Invented an elixir, a fountain–of–youth tonic!

A HOUSE NOT HER OWN

Anne H. Norris

MARTHA stood at the top of the staircase and sighed as she looked down at the magnificent rooms on either side of the center hall. For four years her family had lived here, since the spring of 1861 when her son had answered the call for men to fight in defense of the newly established Confederacy. Never had she dreamed of living in such spacious surroundings. She still was awed by the fourteen-foot ceilings and the tall windows through which she could step onto the porches that wrapped around the sides and front of the house. Yet to her this was nothing more than just the place where she and Lawrence and their children had been living for the past four years. It was not her home, nor did she have any desire for such splendor. She longed to be back in Todd County, Kentucky, in the little house Lawrence had built for her when they were married more than 33 years ago.

Martha never had wanted to be anything except the wife of Lawrence Hall and the mother of his children. Life had been good on their little farm. The boys, Richard and James, had worked with their father in the fields. Their oldest daughter had married her childhood sweetheart and had given them a grandson who was a delight beyond measure.

Her family had been so closely knit. She had thought nothing could ever come between her and her brothers and their extended families. They had worked together and played together. There had been barn-raisings and quilting parties, hay-balings and square dances. Decades earlier they had built the little white frame church where they all gathered every Sunday for worship services.

The last four years had been painful. First there were arguments and angry debates among members of her family concerning southern nationalism. Her brothers had taken a strong stand against slavery, while her Lawrence held fast to his opposing convictions. With the election of Abraham Lincoln to the Presidency, the gulf between them had widened. It still was difficult for Martha to accept the fact that the ones she loved so dearly had become virtual enemies in the great Civil War, brother fighting against brother.

Their son Richard had just celebrated his twentieth birthday when the war began. How well she remembered that morning at breakfast when he had announced that he was leaving to join Morgan's Kentucky Raiders, the cavalry unit led by General John Hunt Morgan. The little girls had cried and begged him not to go. Her own hot tears had dampened her pillow many nights, but Lawrence had been proud of their son. No doubt he himself would have volunteered had it not been that he was needed to care for his family, especially now that both neighbors and kin felt them to be traitors.

The decision to move south had not been an easy one, but even the children were being affected by their brother's departure. The school where once they had looked forward to attending had become a dreaded place where they were taunted by the other boys and girls.

Martha remembered how heavy her heart was as she had packed their personal belongings and what furniture and household items they were able to bring with them. The wagon had been so heavily loaded, she wondered how the horses had been able to pull it. It was an exciting adventure for the children, but what a heartbreaking experience for her—and for Lawrence too.

They were tired and in need of baths when they arrived in Memphis and were most fortunate to have found a place to rent. The 10–room house on the 5,000–acre plantation was available only because the owners did not wish to live so far out from the city in such turbulent times. The house was only nine years old, having been built in 1852 by Samuel and Joseph Mosby. With a brick foundation, weatherboard siding and a slate-covered gable roof, it was both eye–catching and durable.

Although Martha had never met Mrs. Mosby, she felt a certain kinship, both having left their homes because of the war. Maybe soon they could return.

The war was over now. General Lee had surrendered. If only she would receive some word from Richard. He had been wounded in the Battle of Vicksburg and had spent 18 months imprisoned in Rock Island, Ill. Some months earlier they had received a letter from one of his fellow inmates, informing them that Richard was being moved to Richmond, Va. as an exchange prisoner. They had heard nothing more.

Martha wondered if she should begin packing for the trip back to Kentucky. How would they be accepted by their families and former neighbors? Would Richard expect to find them still in Memphis or in Todd County? Had he been given a release?

These were questions that seemed to have no answers.

As she wiped a tear on the corner of her apron, she prayed for divine guidance in the decisions she and Lawrence must make very soon.

It was while she was yet standing at the top of the staircase that the front door was slowly opened. Although Martha was not one to be easily frightened, a chill ran down her spine as she faced the tall young man. His clothing was dirty, tattered, and hanging loosely from his thin body. A heavy dark beard concealed most of his face and his shoulder–length hair hung in a mass of tangles. As he stared up into her face, his eyes glistened and the corners of his mouth turned up in a slight smile. There was something familiar about this man, yet Martha did not recognize him. It was old Sport who ran to greet his master, barking joyfully to welcome him home.

Richard had made the long walk from Richmond, Virginia to Memphis. He was home at last from a war that had not ended as he had wished. He was, nevertheless, more fortunate than many. Some of his friends had lost arms or legs; others had lost their lives.

Martha ran down the stairs with outreached arms. The tears streaming down her face were those of joy and thanksgiving for the return of Richard Robert Redford Hall, her son—my grandfather.

A TIME OF SACRIFICES

Rita Bernero West

IT WAS a time of Four Roses, ration stamps, gas shortages and no nylons. It was World War II, and it was the summer of 1943. My parents yearned for the things they had taken for granted before. They were patriotic, however, and walked to blackout parties and card games, did without sugar in their coffee, and bought War Bonds. My mother applied Max Factor leg makeup and then drew a seam down the back.

There were only two things I felt deprived of at that time. I longed for bubble gum and the opportunity to carry my tonsils around preserved in a jar of formaldehyde. The reason I wanted the bubble gum was obvious; I was eight years old. A tonsillectomy had nothing to do with the war, of course, but when my best friend Jo Carolyn did this at the end of the last school year, it easily made her the most popular girl in the class.

Everyone wanted to walk home from school with her so that they could occasionally gaze at the mysterious mass in the jar. Even though Jo Carolyn lost her long, golden curls in this operation, that aspect didn't alarm me. I already had short, straight dark hair and bangs like the kids on the Campbell Soup cans.

I began that magical summer with those two wistful dreams, along with a crush on Bobby, a boy my age who lived down the street, and who was one of Jo Carolyn's admirers. I felt that if I had some tonsils in a jar and bubble gum, which I'd share with Bobby, then he would be mine. Bobby, however, wasn't remotely interested in me. In fact, he was sort of mean.

When all of the children on the block played War, as we did every day that summer when it didn't rain, Bobby "shot" me by hurling more hard, green Chinaberries at me than anyone else. Depending on how many of us were playing on any given day, there were always three bad guys—one Hitler, one Tojo, and one Mussolini. The rest were American soldiers and sailors. Bobby always pointed out that I had to be Mussolini because I was the only one with an Italian surname. I proudly bore this dubious title throughout the summer, even though I was shot and killed multiple times.

Going to the movies on Saturday afternoons was really special. Bobby would sit in the row directly behind me and kick my seat throughout two full-length movies, a cartoon, a newsreel, a serial, and a Pete Smith Specialty. Occasionally, he'd lean forward and snatch a handful of popcorn out of my nickel bag.

Many days a bunch of us would decide to roller-skate. We'd take our keys, tighten our sidewalk skates, and take off to go around the block. At some point Bobby always wanted to race. He would, of course, pull ahead of me and then stop suddenly so that I would run into him and fall. I was never without scrapes on my knees, and I was intensely proud of them.

Bobby made fun of my Brownie Scout uniform. He laughed at my piano recitals, and vowed he'd never come near me again when I had measles and there was a quarantine sign on our front door.

Near the end of the summer, my little brother and Bobby and I were playing by ourselves in Bobby's back yard. They were both more or less ignoring me and talking about BB guns, identifying fighter planes, and general boy talk of the time. Without warning, Bobby turned to my brother and yelled, "Do you dare me to kiss your sister?" He made it sound comparable to eating a worm or an equally disgusting feat. My brother was gleeful. "Yeah! Do it!"

I began to run. Bobby tackled me and I went to the ground. He pinned my hands down and smacked me right on the mouth. My brother was laughing and dancing about. I was prepared for Bobby to shriek something like "Phooey!" and then spit on the ground. Instead, he looked at me quizzically a second, threw his head back, and there it was. Bobby uttered, what was to me, the ultimate compliment of the time. "Hubba! Hubba!"

Nothing had prepared me for this. I spent what was left of that marvelous summer mooning over Bobby, although he never attempted to kiss me again. He simply continued to tease and pester me as usual.

At the end of August, Bobby and his family moved to California and I never heard from or saw him again. I started back to school without the bubble gum or my tonsils in a jar, but it didn't matter. I had so, so much more. I had experienced, just like in the movies, a wartime romance.

BETWEEN THE GRACE NOTES

Madge H. Lewis

AS THE 747 thundered up toward the ominous carpet of clouds, Julia squeezed her eyes shut and wrapped her arms around her oversized travel purse.

"Peg?" Julia's throat constricted as she tried to speak. The hoarse whisper brought no response. Julia opened her mouth to speak again, but the plane lurched and the acceleration caused her to push even further against the back of the seat. Were they crashing? Was the engine sputtering? Could they take her back? She willed herself not to scream. There was nothing in the Orient worth this.

Peg, the tour escort who sat next to her, patted her arm. "Don't worry," she consoled. "I haven't lost a client in the twenty years I've been in business. Everyone is nervous on the first flight." The noise of the motor lessened and the plane leveled off. Julia heard the popping of a cork and opened her eyes. The seat belt sign was off and a smiling stewardess was standing beside her taking drink orders. Peg ordered a Coke, then turned to Julia. "Now, you can relax. Have a little toddy. Perhaps that will settle your nerves."

"I don't drink, thank you." Julia knew she sounded prim and severe but she couldn't help it—she was trying to cover her confusion. She became aware of a long strand of dark hair, streaked with gray, hanging across the corner of her left eye. She retrieved the hairpins that had fallen out when she had tried to meld into the seat for takeoff, and tucked the hair back into the bun where it belonged. "Why are we spending the night in Anchorage? Why doesn't the itinerary take us directly to Tokyo?"

"Adding Alaska to an Orient itinerary breaks up the travel time into more reasonable segments. Also, it provides a contrast to our overnight stop in Honolulu on the way home."

Otto Malone, one of the eight male members of the group of twenty, came to stand beside Peg's seat. "It looks like we have an interesting crowd." He chuckled, then added. "Are we going to have Happy Hour in your suite before dinner—like we usually do on your trips?"

"Indeed we are," Peg replied.

Julia knew she would never fit in, especially at a gathering referred to casually as "Happy Hour." These people were either long time friends or had become relaxed with each other at the Memphis airport where the tour had originated. And to top it off, this man—this clown—gaily flung back the words, "Aren't we having fun?" as he left the aisle to let the stewardesses get by to serve drinks.

Fun? thought Julia as her stomach lurched when the plane hit an air pocket. I'd rather be home getting ready to go to work at the telephone company—to a job I thought I hated for thirty years. She looked at the gold retirement pin on her lapel. For the first time, she felt a warm glow for the company that had been her mainstay all her adult life and that had helped her support her invalid mother until her death last year. Even her mother's complaints were preferable to this plane business.

"Otto is a successful businessman today," Peg interrupted her negative thoughts. "But he was an Arthur Murray dance instructor when he was young. He goes on many of the trips I escort. We have live music in many of the dining rooms where we stay on our tours and it makes the ladies feel special when he asks them to dance."

Julia shut her eyes again. If there was one thing worse than crashing, it was the thought of being propelled around a dance floor—especially by a man who had been a professional instructor. The one time she had ventured onto a dance floor was during her high school graduation prom. Even then, she had danced only with her brother who was aware of her shyness and had offered to escort her. She was taller than most of the boys and no one else had asked her to dance.

When the plane touched down at Anchorage the group disembarked and clambered onto their private bus for the transfer to their hotel. Julia remembered that Peg had warned her that single rooms at the "Anchorage Westward" were clean and adequate, but not deluxe, so there was no disappointment when she saw the Spartan furnishings—only the relief of being back on earth and the blessed feeling of aloneness.

Julia's relief was interrupted by the shrill sound of the telephone. Peg's voice responded to her "Hello."

"Julia, we're going to meet in Suite 405 for drinks at 6:30. I'll have orange juice for you and the others who don't care for alcohol. It will be casual and informal—we perch on the beds, sit on the floor, and lounge on any available chair. Then, we'll go to the dining room together. See you at 6:30."

Julia heard the click of the phone before she could protest and when she tried to call Peg back, the line was busy. Her lovely dream of dinner served in her room came to an abrupt halt. She was too polite to hurt Peg's feelings by failing to show up.

With a heavy heart she went to her first Happy Hour.

She found a spot on the edge of one of the beds and squeezed in between two ladies—Marge and Leila. She sat stiffly, sipping her orange juice, observing the others: the couples who seemed to have such full lives, the single women who were alone, as she was, but who, unlike her, appeared to have fallen right in with the crowd; and then there was Otto. He busied himself acting as majordomo, bartender, and life of the party.

"Let me freshen up your drink with a dash of vodka," he said, holding the bottle toward Julia. "You'll be surprised how it will pep up your drink—and you, too, after the second dash."

"No, thank you," she replied and held her hand over the rim of her glass. Otto gave her a quizzical look and continued on his rounds to the other guests.

The isolation of Happy Hour was repeated in Tokyo at the elegant Imperial Hotel, in Hakone at the little country inn at the foot of Mt. Fuji, in Kyoto at the impressive Miyako. During the daytime tours the loneliness was intensified when Julia wanted to turn to someone and share her admiration of the Buddhist and Shinto shrines, to join with the others in the pleasure of the ancient tea ceremony, to stroll companionably with another member of the group through a serene Japanese garden. Instead she walked apart, listening to them make plans to get their hair done, to get manicures, to go back to that quaint shop where there were such beautiful *obis* for fantastic prices.

Their last night in Japan, Otto, dressed in a kimono he had purchased that day, pretended that Happy Hour was a tea ceremony and he made bows and took mincing steps that sent the group into gales of laughter. When he reached Julia, he bowed low and said in a high-pitched voice, "Would missy like lime splash—a non–alcoholic drink concocted by humble servant?"

Even Julia had to laugh and surprised herself by using the Japanese words for "Thank you very much" she had learned that day, "Arigato gozaimasu," and held her glass out to him. "Just a taste, please. Really, no more than a dash."

"Frosty lime splash. Missy get dash." Otto carefully poured a small amount of the limeade over ice and stood back to watch her taste it. "How missy like?"

"Very good." To her surprise, it was good: tangy, yet sweet, and the bubbles from the cold sparkling lime mix tickled her nose. From then on, Otto fixed her a frosty lime splash at Happy Hour.

Days blurred into a brilliant kaleidoscope of Taiwan, Singapore, Bangkok and Hong Kong. When their transfer bus pulled into the circular drive in front of the venerable Peninsula Hotel in Kowloon, Hong Kong, the women could hardly wait for Peg to give them their room keys so they could begin shopping.

As Julia waited for her key, Leila said to her in passing, "We're going to boost the economy on Nathan Road. Wish you could lend me those comfortable SAS shoes you have on. We'll be dead on our feet when we get back." The sound of their laughter floated back to her, and she had a sense of time leaving her behind.

After Julia received her key from Peg, she walked alone through the shopping arcade of the hotel. The clothes in the windows presented an intoxicating tapestry of color: pale blue, soft rose, vibrant green, golden yellow. She had never imagined that such finery existed and that she would be surrounded by it on every side.

A mannequin, about her height, seemed to be looking right at her. The mannequin was smiling, holding one jeweled arm out as though to lure her inside. She was robed in a silk dress, glistening in purples and blues. Next to the mannequin was her own reflection, a ghost, shapeless in a wrinkled, polyester travel suit, standing aloof, unsmiling. No one would approach that ghost, in part because she seemed so independent, so superior, so—distant. Julia looked at the happy dummy who was too smart to rebuff friendly overtures; she would participate happily in parties. Julia realized she had retreated into a world of her own making. Perhaps, she thought, if I liked myself better, I could be more outgoing and receptive.

She called Peg's suite when she reached her room. The beat of her heart matched the strident ringing tones of the telephone. "Peg," she spoke quickly before all resolve could abandon her, "I need your help while we're in Hong Kong."

"What can I do for you?"

"I'd like to buy a new blouse and—and perhaps some new shoes. I might even get my hair cut. Will you have some time to spend with me?"

"Of course. We'll have fun. I'm going to have some things made by Chang Lee, my favorite tailor. Let's meet downstairs and spend the afternoon together. See you in the lobby in thirty minutes."

Peg hung up before Julia could change her mind. They met and started on their quest. Peg knew exactly where to go and how to talk to the wily Chinese merchants. She helped Julia select a ready–made, pale gold floral blouse and coral skirt, as well as a beautiful light green gossamer fabric with matching underlining for evening wear, a black wool crepe for a suit that could be changed about with other skirts and blouses, and material for a teal blue shift with a jewel neckline.

"But, Peg, I only wanted a blouse. What will I do with these clothes you've picked out?" Julia protested.

"Enjoy them. You can show everyone at home what great bargains you got. Now, let's head for Henry Wang's." Peg ignored Julia's feeble protests, and her excitement came through in the breathless way she spoke. "He makes shoes and, believe it or not, they will be ready by tomorrow. He'll also have purses to match. Then we'll head for the jewelry shop. You need a nice string of pearls to go with your new outfits. Now, perk up! Aren't we having fun? Oh, there I go, sounding just like Otto."

Julia was unwittingly caught up in the excitement of the moment. "What about getting my hair done? I know you'll find this hard to believe, but I've never been to a beauty parlor."

"We'll go to one tomorrow. Then you can throw away those hairpins. You're never going to need them again!"

There was no Happy Hour that night. Everyone was out shopping. They returned in time for a late dinner, and Julia appeared in her new blouse and skirt. She couldn't help but overhear Frank Barton, a handsome patrician with white hair, whisper to his wife, "I think our shrinking violet is beginning to bloom." Julia's face reddened but she smiled inwardly and sat next to them, entering into conversation with Mrs. Barton.

When the music began, Otto was the first one on the dance floor with one of the single girls. Julia's pulse leapt in her throat as he approached her when the next piece began.

"How about a whirl around the dance floor?" he asked, drawing her to her feet.

She hoped he didn't sense the fear in her voice. "I'm sorry. I don't know how to dance."

"Well, I'm known around the world as 'dance instructor at large.' Let's give it a try."

Julia felt completely disembodied as she reached the dance floor.

"I'll give you a short lesson—then we'll show these other tourists how it's really done," Otto said as he placed his arm around her. "The first thing you must do is relax and keep your eyes off the floor. Bear in mind that your right foot is queen and the man's is the opposite—his left foot is king. Remember, the man always leads. When he executes a move, whether it's forward, backward, to the side, turn, pivot or balance, this is always done with the man's left foot, which mean's right foot for the woman. If you remember these two things, you'll be able to dance well when the trip is over."

"I'll try," Julia said. Her whole body was quivering. The band went into a slow waltz. She stepped on Otto's left foot. He smiled. She stumbled. He smiled more. At first it was one stumble for each measure, then every other measure. By the middle of the dance she hadn't stepped on Otto's foot through two whirls. When the last note faded, she reluctantly dropped her arms and resisted the urge to ask him to dance again.

"You were great—my best pupil on the trip," Otto said gallantly as he led her back to her table at the end of the waltz.

"Thank you, Otto. I learned a lot." She doubted he would ever ask her to dance again. He couldn't have enjoyed having his feet trounced. Had she made a fool of herself?

On their last day in Hong Kong, Julia and Peg went to the beauty salon for a facial and manicure and hair styling. The smells of the hair spray, the nail polish, the perfumed ointments introduced Julia into a new and exciting world. Peg gave instructions to Julia's stylist for a short haircut and a light auburn rinse.

Julia relaxed until she sat before the mirror and knew that she was about to lose the mass of long hair that had never before been cut. The shorn locks piled up higher and higher on the floor around them. She felt naked, thinking of Samson and how he had lost his strength when his hair was cut. Would she ever be herself again? She closed her eyes and was glad her mother was not here to see it.

As Julia sat under the dryer a tear trickled down her cheeks for the kind of person she had been, the wasted years, the sublimation of her own desires. She had lived up to the responsibilities that had been thrust upon her but—what about now? Would she emerge from this experience with the capacity for fun and the give–and–take of friendships?

When her hair had been combed and the chair turned for her to get the full view of herself in the mirror, Julia shed another tear—this time from happiness. Her hair had been shaped into a smooth cap to accentuate the fine bone structure in her face and the auburn rinse which covered the gray brought out the green in her eyes; she had forgotten they were green. And her skin! The makeup enhanced the fair color of her skin, and it looked almost like porcelain.

Julia rushed to the shops to pick up her new finery and to the hotel to dress for dinner.

She chose her green dress; the ivory shoes and bag, the lustrous pearls at her ears and throat provided an elegant touch. She picked up her gold retirement pin and held it against the green of the dress. "Not tonight, old buddy, you don't match. You may never match again!" She put the pin in her jewelry case and with a chuckle, she dropped, one by one, the oversized hairpins into the waste basket.

She took one last look at herself in the mirror. She saw a tall, slender auburn–haired woman with a slight smile. She looked as good as the dummy in the window! She laughed and almost sprinted to the dining room where she sat next to the Bartons. Once again, Frank turned to his wife and said, "Well, my dear, I was right. She was budding before, but I believe she is now in full bloom. You look absolutely splendid, Miss Julia!"

The waiter poured champagne and toasts were drunk to Peg, to the group, to the manager of the Peninsula Hotel, to the fabulous fairy–tale colony of Hong Kong and to Julia's shocked surprise, even to her. She was beginning to feel giddy from excitement when Otto asked her to dance. This time she arose and extended her hand to his without a qualm.

"I remember," she said as they started dancing, "Your right foot is king."

"No, no, you have it backward. It's—" Then he laughed as he realized that she had been joking.

Julia followed Otto's lead easily, in spite of the slight awkwardness of new shoes. The music buoyed her movements and she had no problem keeping time She could feel the swirl of her new green dress around her legs as Otto led her gracefully into the turns. She heard the members of the group applaud as they swept past the table. Happiness and excitement were waiting for her. Like the mannequin in the window, she need only stretch out a hand.

HARD ROCK

Ethel Joyner

A vision the likes of which I've never seen
Jolted me as I sat before the TV screen.
My eyes became more riveted as I sat amazed
Watching these creatures become more crazed.

Castoff clothes, strange hats, guitars to the knee,
They bounced in unison to an electronic cacophony.
As the decibels mounted an assault to the ear,
The thought came to me: Will I ever again hear?

Blaring into the microphones, the lyrics ajumbled,
I strove for the message, hopelessly mumbled.
Adding to the confusion, the din and the blare,
Was a roar from the audience, arms waving midair.

A generational gap exists, of this I am aware.
I dream of the forties from my old rocking chair.
Of the graveyard's population, it can be said
They've been delivered; they're the grateful dead.

MY HUSBAND, THE NEAT FREAK

Anne H. Norris

MY HUSBAND Norman and I are living proof that opposites attract. He is a dyed–in–the–wool neat freak. I am having a good day if my socks match.

I spotted Norman when he walked into the room where men and women I didn't recognize were gathering for our 35th high school reunion. He wore a blue-and-white striped shirt that was void of the slightest wrinkle. His trousers were perfectly creased and his shoes looked as if they had been given more attention than I had spent on my entire weekend wardrobe. He was totally neat, and he was single!

Norman was no longer the skinny boy with red hair and freckles that I vaguely remembered from our ninth-grade math class. His hair had darkened over the years, the freckles had somewhat faded, and his slender six-foot frame gave credibility to the rumor that he could be found most weekdays on the golf course. I liked what I saw. Before the evening was over he had accepted my dinner invitation, albeit with a bit of hesitation. I don't know why men are so suspicious of such innocent acts of kindness.

My qualifications as a contender for this prize specimen were limited, but I had a few things in my favor. I had been widowed twelve years earlier when my three children were teenagers. Now they were all out of the nest and urging their mother to feather it again. Added to this was my expertise in the kitchen. I knew the way to a man's heart was through his stomach and I was planning a direct cardiac route before Mr. Neatnik ever had a hunger pain.

The first real clue I had as to Norman's total commitment to neatness came when he arrived at my house for dinner. If he had come directly from the dealer's showroom, his car could not have looked better. No dents. No bents. No smudges. No bugs on the windshield. No bird had dared to fly over his car.

I had an uneasy feeling that I may have been a little hasty with the dinner invitation. Norman probably didn't allow dust balls under his furniture, but surely he would understand that I couldn't throw out last week's newspapers until I had time to read the obituaries. It was just that removing the month's accumulation from the kitchen counters, and putting away the laundry that I didn't finish over the weekend because of the reunion, had taken more time than I had anticipated. I did regret, however, that the costumes my grandchildren had worn two weeks earlier in the Fourth of July parade were still piled on the end of the living room sofa.

But love is blind, and this wonderful man did not seem to notice that I tend to be somewhat less than neat. I felt confident that in time I could help him overcome this obsession for neatness and we would be able to strike a happy medium. It was a leap year and I leapt. Four months later we were married.

We began our life together in the house where I had lived for fifteen years. I had not realized so many improvements were needed. For the next three years Norman had little time for golf. First he tackled the garage. He built work benches and installed shelving and peg boards. There was no way he could begin a project without adequate space to work and easy accessibility to his tools. Next came the renovation of our bedroom closet. He installed new rods for hanging shorter garments above the existing rods, shelves for hats and such, and racks for all our shoes. The finished product was remarkable. Our closet space was doubled. But try as I might, I couldn't keep my side as tidy as his. It was difficult to keep my shoes lined up orderly on the little shelves when I was in the habit of opening the closet door and kicking them inside. Norman never complained. When the floor was so littered with my shoes that the door wouldn't close, he would pick them up and put them neatly on the racks.

Finally I was getting accustomed to all the new shelves and cabinets and learning where I could hide half–eaten candy bars when we decided to buy another house. Norman had to start over again. First the garage and workshop. Then the closets with extra rods and rows of shoe racks. We closed on an early afternoon and by that evening everything was in its proper place. Dishes were in the cabinets, books on the shelves. Even our pictures were hung at the carefully measured height and most suitable wall position.

Within three months Norman had painted the outside of the house. The original color did not blend with the shingles on the roof.

Our lawn soon looked better than the greens at the golf course, which Norman saw less of now than when he was single. He fertilized, watered, trimmed, edged and mowed. If a weed dared to show its ugly head, its days were numbered. We had the showplace of the neighborhood for three years. Then we moved again.

It's hard to believe we have been in our present home more than six years. Last summer Norman replaced the back deck. I was his apprentice. I had two major responsibilities. I pulled all the nails out of the old boards as he pried them up, just to lessen the possibility of anyone stepping on a nail before the boards could be disposed of. My other job was to hold a spacer between the boards as each was screwed to the foundation to assure that the space between every board was exactly the same. There are no nails in our new deck. Only screws, all in perfect lines. Of course Norman personally selected every piece of lumber to be sure it wasn't warped or didn't have excessive knotholes.

The winter months are the worst for Norman. He is running out of inside things that need his neat touch. He has made new shelves in the utility room so the soft drinks can be properly stored and not left on the floor where I have always put them. He built book shelves, floor to ceiling, across one end of our living room. The walk-in closet in our bedroom could be featured in "Home Beautiful" if my side were not always in disarray.

Last week when I was putting away the laundry, I opened Norman's sock drawer and saw that my neat freak had been at it again. His cold-weather socks were neatly stacked, by colors, in the front of the drawer and the ones he wears during the summer months had been moved to the back. His underwear drawer was equally as neat—V–neck undershirts in one stack, round–neck undershirts in another, shorts neatly folded and stacked in one corner. Not wanting to inadvertently put his socks or underwear in the wrong stack, I left his things on the bed. Better for him to put them away than me since I don't have much experience with folding and stacking.

To be sure, there are many advantages to having a neatnik husband. Norman has taken over a lot of the household chores. I praise him for how well he vacuums the carpet and dusts the furniture, and I assure him that he irons much better than I. My fear is that this may be coming to an end. He no longer has his summer shirts on white hangers, fall clothes on yellow hangers, winter jackets and coats on red, and his spring wardrobe on green.

I really hate to see him change. I love him just the way he is. After all, it was his neatness that first attracted me. But either he is mellowing with age or finally has decided it's more fun on the golf course than in the broom closet.

MY SECRET GARDEN

Ethel Joyner

My secret garden has been lovingly seeded,
Requires no nurturing, will never be weeded.
Nutritionally deprived, no need to feed it.
Overcoming the odds has miraculously succeeded.

Flowers in profusion bloom the year round,
Arising from a depleted, unproductive ground.
It is a miracle; my thumb has never been green.
Folks rave over this visually–stunning scene!

I revel in its beauty, my glorious creation
Inspired by a fertile, overactive imagination.
Disenchantment sets in by the end of the summer
As I survey my garden, in truth, a real bummer!

GRAN'MA'S BLUEBIRD

Ruth Crenshaw

"GRAN'MA sure does love birds. I'll bet she knows more about birds than anybody, even that Mr. Audubon," piped my little brother Daniel in his high pitched, nine–year–old voice.

We three, Daniel, Nathan, and I, were sitting around the table in Gran'ma's kitchen making "Welcome Home" posters for her return from the hospital where she had had hip surgery. Age and arthritis had worn the bone away, and she had finally agreed to hold still for the operation.

"I'm signing my poster from Mr. and Mrs. Robin, 'cause I'll bet they missed her the most, except those pesky blue jays," continued Daniel.

"Nathan, did you put out fresh thistle seeds for the finches?" I asked.

"Yep, I did," Nathan answered, a little defensively. "And I cleaned all the bird baths. Now I'm getting ready to hang the new house in the bluebird tree."

"Sure wish those ole bluebirds would show up this year," it was Daniel again. "Maggie, why do you suppose they never come?"

Actually, my name is Margaret, but the boys started calling me Maggie because they thought Margaret was too snooty to fit me, since I was one of them—partner in all their schemes and escapades.

Hundreds of birds came to Gran'ma's back yard every year, but the ones she most looked for each spring were the tiny bluebirds. And yet none had ever come.

"Maybe they don't like the houses," she would reason.

So she would buy another one and hang it with the rest. She had chosen a tulip poplar with its curved branches and broad, protective leaves to be the bluebirds' tree. The tree was now ornamented with bluebird houses of every shape: round igloo types, Swiss chalets, and one like a real log cabin. The newest one was a miniature blue cottage with shutters at fake windows. All of them had the smallest of openings and were hung high with wire she had greased to deter furry invaders.

Each spring we joined her in watching and waiting to see just one bluebird. Often, sightings had been reported by other members of the Audubon Society and Gran'ma would fume and snort. I'm sure she thought their reports false, since she held the title of champion bird watcher in the group. Yet, somehow I also think she felt defeated at not being able to attract those little bits of blue feathers to her yard.

Since we lived only two blocks from her, we three were at her house as much as our own. Her house and yard were extensions of our schoolroom. She was our teacher; we were her willing pupils. She taught without our knowing we were being taught. If she could get Daniel to sit still while she told the story of John J. Audubon, she was, indeed, a teacher without equal. As a matter of fact, our first lesson in procreation was from a robin's egg which had rolled from the nest. Ever so reverently, Gran'ma held the tiny embryo in her hand and pointed out, "This would have been the head. See the eye there?"

"Where's its beak?" queried Daniel, always full of questions.

"It hasn't formed yet," she explained.

So we grew up in that atmosphere of surprises, miracles, and the wonders of nature. Each changing season was a special time—an unfolding of how things adapt, make their way and endure, thus fulfilling their role in the scheme of life. As the seasons changed there was always excitement in the preparations: bulbs to lift in the fall, cleaning and storing the tools and birdhouses, and cleaning and hanging the dozen feeders for the winter. Then came spring, the busiest of all the seasons.

"What color tulips are we going to plant?" I asked every year.

"Oh, let's plant every color we can find. Weren't the lavender ones pretty last spring?" she would ask, then add, "Maggie, I do believe your thumb is turning green," and give a chuckle as she patted my hand.

Of all the things she taught us, I think the lessons from the birds have been the most lasting. It's true, as Daniel said, "She knew everything about birds!" She knew every bird by its call, all their migratory habits, when the first nest was built, their favorite foods, and which ones mated for life. She helped us translate the mockingbird's song into words, from a poem she had learned as a child. "Listen," she would whisper. "He's going to say, 'Ten-thirty, ten–thirty–potato, potato–hurry now, hurry now, now hurry'." And we listened and believed.

She told us, "The six notes of a song sparrow's call were borrowed by the composer of the song *I'm in Love with you, Honey.* You will hear bars of other melodies in the calls of many birds. After all, they were our first musicians."

Often we stood still while a towhee called to his mate and shared his relief when her plaintive and reassuring call came from the far corner of the thicket. Yet, it was the diminutive but tough bluebird which had shunned Gran'ma's bird haven.

"If Gran'ma keeps buying bluebird houses, she's gonna run out of limbs," said Nathan as he climbed down the ladder. He had become the designated house hanger and retriever since Gran'ma had been forbidden to climb ladders. She, in her eightieth year, however, was still spry and, even with a painful hip, could chase old Sam, the neighbor's cat, from his stalking place.

"What time will Dad and Mom bring Gran'ma home?" asked Daniel. "I've finished my poster."

Then I had a thought. "Listen, fellows, do you suppose we could put one of those imitation bluebirds in one of the houses and fool Gran'ma?"

"Not a chance, Maggie. You couldn't fool Gran'ma with a dumb, fake bird in a million years." Daniel's voice rose with such fervor that for a moment I was convinced my idea was all wet.

"At the Garden Center I saw some pretty realistic birds," I countered. "Maybe they would have a bluebird the right size to fit one of the houses. We could put it in the new one. It's the highest, and with her eyesight she might just think it real."

Daniel laughed, playing the skeptic. "What's she gonna' think when it just sits there all day. Even when they're on the nest they have to eat. How can you explain that to Gran'ma? Say it's on a diet?"

Glancing at his watch, Nathan finally answered Daniel's question, "Dad said that it might be after four when the doctor discharges her. It's now one forty–five. We'll have time to make it to the Garden Center and check out those birds. Bluebirds may come to visit Gran'ma after all!" I noticed a tinge of excitement in his usual matter-of-fact demeanor. "Listen, Daniel, you stay here and put up the signs. You have my permission to put yours in the front yard."

Luck was with us that day. We found an almost perfect specimen. I held it up while Nathan stood back to scrutinize from all angles. "If only the head shows, we may just pull this off, don't you think, Maggie?"

"If we don't, Gran'ma will just laugh and enjoy the joke," I reassured him. "She has that keen sense of humor."

When we got back we found Daniel hopping with excitement. "Nathan! Maggie! I've found a way to make the fake bird move. I'll tie this fishing line around its neck and after Gran'ma looks at it a little, I'll jerk it back inside the birdhouse. With another line I can pull it back out later." His words tumbled over each other in his enthusiasm.

Our plan of action complete, Nathan climbed the tulip poplar and deposited the trussed–up bird with its pin–head eyes and glued–down wings which would never take to the wind. Never mind, this imitation–of–life had taken on an important role—to fool Gran'ma into a bit of happiness. Carefully Daniel straightened his fishing lines and we waited, our conspiracy binding us more closely together.

When Gran'ma arrived home, everyone was talking at once. She couldn't wait to get to her birds and to try out her walker in the back yard. Mother was cautioning that she was to stay out only a few minutes and not get excited. Nathan grabbed Gran'ma's old canvas hat off the rack and put it, slightly askew, on her head. She smiled up at him as the little group escorted her into her familiar haunt.

The yard was alive with birds! It seemed every bird in the neighborhood had gathered for the homecoming. There were chickadees, tufted titmice, cardinals, and even a shy creeper had joined the company. To make the welcome complete, a rust-headed cowbird with its quick, sweet notes sang a prelude for a mockingbird, high in a cottonwood, to commence a recitation of his entire vocabulary.

At just that moment, Gran'ma looked up toward the bluebird tree. "Oh," she whispered, "a bluebird!"

Daniel pulled his invisible line and the little fake moved out of sight. As he pulled the other line there was a flash of blue and we stood transfixed as we watched a real bluebird alight on the roof of the birdhouse. I looked at Gran'ma's face. There was a light of purest bliss as tears came in her eyes.

"At last, bluebirds have come," she said. "Oh! Oh! How grand, how beautiful! They have come, children!"

Our mother, afraid Gran'ma was getting too tired, called us inside. Gran'ma was still smiling when we kissed her good-bye. We were a happy trio on our way home.

"It was that little ole fake that brought the bluebirds," declared Daniel. "Do you think we fooled Gran'ma?"

"I don't know," said Nathan. "Maybe. Anyway, I'm glad we did it."

At three o'clock the next morning we were awakened by the telephone. It was Mother saying that Gran'ma had suffered a stroke. Our Gran'ma was dead.

That afternoon we filed into the funeral home to say good-bye. Our parents stepped back from the casket to make room for the three of us. With a tear-streaked face and stifling a sob, Daniel reached over, unfolded Gran'ma's hand, then re-folded her fingers around the tiny fake bird. "Maybe it will bring the bluebirds to Gran'ma's back yard in heaven," he said in a hoarse whisper. "Then she will be happy there, too."

ADELAIDE

Ann J. Huckaba

WHEN my husband John received word from his receptionist that he was to go immediately to the doctor's office across the hall, he knew there was an emergency and Dr. Billingsly needed help. His reaction was automatic and, leaving his own patients, he rushed out the door. His thoughts raced, wondering what the emergency could be. For all practical purposes Dr. Billingsly was retired, but like many men who have worked long years, he found it difficult to give up a place to go each morning. His wife Adelaide who had been his assistant for forty years, made the daily trek with him to the office. Occasionally a long time patient would come by for some minor attention and Dr. Billingsly would willingly attend him, but the office really served as a place to take care of personal business.

My husband assumed one of those infrequent patients had come in and was in some emergency condition—therefore, the call for help. Or perhaps Dr. Billingsly himself was having some physical problem.

When John rushed through the door, there stood Adelaide behind the desk looking through some packages.

"Where is Dr. Billingsly and what is wrong?" my husband asked.

Adelaide informed him Dr. Billingsly was not in and that she wanted to show John what she had purchased for her husband. She proceeded to open a package to display some fine underwear from the best men's store in the city. She explained that she wanted John to see what good care she took of Dr. Billingsly. John explained as nicely as his irritation would allow that he had left a patient, others were waiting, and he must leave. When she petulantly objected he felt obliged to at least look at her purchases.

Adelaide was not old enough to be senile but was certainly old enough to be demanding and rather eccentric. This was displayed in many ways, and more and more as time went by. She had placed some rather nice Victorian furniture in the reception room—things she had no place to keep at home. To be sure that no one sat on the chairs and sofa, she put big poster–board signs on the seats that read: "Do Not Sit Here!"—which would discourage anyone calling at the office, especially patients.

Adelaide evidently loved a battle. She had a running feud with the post office over the location of a mail box on the street by the building, and was constantly after the laboratory delivery trucks regarding the temporary parking in the drive at the building's entrance. The basement parking garage employees had their share of her biting complaints, and she was forever at odds with the building management, especially the maintenance crew.

Late one afternoon I met John at his office and, when leaving, we saw Adelaide through her open door. She insisted we come in for a visit—and what a strange visit it was! Her conversation was all about the good care she gave Dr. Billingsly. She had just bought new shirts for him and wanted us to see how fine they were. Her husband contributed very little to the conversation but did not once agree or disagree with her. To show what a great job she had done in taking care of Dr. Billingsly, she took us back to his private office for the ultimate proof. There on the wall was a very large frame with glass–covered matted pictures of his medical school graduating class. With a red marking crayon she had made a big check mark on the glass over the face of each physician as he passed on to another world. Only Dr. Billingsly and four others remained unmarked.

I could not believe Adelaide would routinely do this, right there in Dr. Billingsly's office where every day he faced the picture on the wall across from his desk. John and I mentioned the picture from time to time, and though we both thought it was morbidly funny, we agreed it was a little too grim.

Some months later Adelaide again called John from her office to come immediately. Of course, he was not going to fall for that again and insisted he be told what the problem was. If it was not an emergency, he could not leave his patients, but would come over at the end of the day.

When he entered Dr. Billingsly's office late that afternoon, Adelaide was in a huff and spoke only to inform him that if John had called, Dr. Billingsly would have gone to him at once. John tried to tell her it was a busy afternoon, and he could not leave just for incidental conversation. On her desk was an open box filled with beautiful wool socks, no doubt her most recent evidence of the fine care she gave Dr. Billingsly and the object of her emergency call to John.

That was the last time Adelaide ever spoke to my husband, always ignoring his greeting and turning her head when they met in the hall.

Some months later Adelaide passed away quietly after a short illness. Dr. Billingsly was truly at a loss. He closed his office and moved all the contents to an already overcrowded apartment. For several years he spent much time and ate most evening meals at our house. Then, suffering the ills of advanced age, he joined Adelaide at their final resting place.

John and I were asked to assist in sorting and clearing out the clutter from Dr. Billingsly's apartment. In going through the boxes, still packed for their removal from his office years before, I came upon the large photograph of his graduating class. I spent some time looking over those pictures of physicians whose lives were spent in the care of others. I recalled so clearly the afternoon Adelaide showed us the photograph of her husband's medical graduating class and the proud credit she took for Dr. Billingsly being one of the members still alive.

I rummaged through a nearby desk until I found what I was looking for, then sat down with that frame of pictures in front of me. In tribute to an irascible, but determined, Adelaide and her complete confidence that only her special care assured longevity, I carefully placed a matching red check mark over the one remaining photograph from that large class.

THE AGES OF WOMAN

Madge H. Lewis

IN THE youth of middle age, I became a travel consultant, a title which seemed to have more panache than "travel agent" and considerably more than "a clerk who sells airline tickets." I had yet to learn that a title must be earned and that travel entails more than destinations.

No experience qualifies one for the title of "consultant" in the field of travel until one has traveled. Nothing takes the place of saying to one's client, "You really should choose this itinerary. Let me tell you about some of my experiences on this same tour last year."

During the early stages of my career, my duties involved traveling to Europe in the winter to make advance group bookings at hotels. European hotels could not accommodate the vast crowds of Americans who set siege to its capitals from early spring to late fall and for that reason the agency reserved rooms far in advance. Deregulation of the airlines had not yet taken place and the golden era of the travel industry was at its peak!

After one of these demanding assignments, I took a three day holiday in Switzerland. That year my business trip ended in Geneva two weeks before Christmas. I boarded the train to Visp where I changed to the narrow–gauge railroad that transported me higher and higher to the fairy tale village of Zermatt in the Alps.

The train came to a stop at dusk. December snow fell in big fluffy flakes. An enterprising Swiss lad had set up a stall near the station and the smell of bratwurst sizzling on his grill filled the air. The skiers, coming in from their day's activity, crowded around him, unable to bypass the tantalizing aroma.

The tourist director of the village maintained the traditional policy permitting no motor–driven vehicles within town limits, thus creating an atmosphere quite different from the streets of other cities. The hotel management had arranged for me to be met by a sleigh pulled by a prancing horse, his nostrils flaring, breathing smoke into the cold air, the bells on his harness jingling a merry tune.

After the coachman loaded my luggage, we started down the narrow street which is the heart and soul of Zermatt. Hotels and elegant shops lined both sides, and in the background, as the mountains sloped higher, small houses nestled, smoke rising from every chimney. Christmas decorations adorned doorways and windows and never before or since have I felt the spirit of the season so deeply as I did that snowy night.

The horses clip–clopped their way down the short stretch to my hotel, which lay at the far end of the street. Halfway along, a sign affixed to the side of a building bore the ominous message to the skiers who flocked to the village: "Broken bones repaired here."

Tourists walked along beside us heading for their hotels after an active day on the slopes. They spoke many different languages, creating a cacophony of sound, laughing as they munched on their bratwurst.

When the sleigh stopped in front of my hotel, I looked up for the first time at the huge and gracefully curved Matterhorn rising like a pyramid from the mountains around it. The magnificence of it took my breath away. No wonder it was called "the mountain of mountains!"

I left the sleigh reluctantly to go into the hotel, wanting to stay outside and drink in the beauty that surrounded me. I was reminded of the words of Goethe—he surely must have been here when he wrote them: "I would say to the moment, linger awhile. Thou art so fair."

I entered the old fashioned, but luxurious hotel that had been accommodating the public since the last half of the nineteenth century. The reception clerk greeted me and sent me on my way to a spacious room. There was barely enough time to bathe and change for dinner.

When I reached the dining room, the maitre d' escorted me to a table where I had a full view of the room and the other guests. I admired the grandeur that surrounded me, the crystal chandeliers, the windows draped on the side with burgundy velvet trimmed in golden fringe, the vast expanse left clear so the view of the Matterhorn would not be impeded. I remember it all so clearly—the colors, the textures, the way it smelled of freshly baked bread and cheese fondue.

Near the entrance the maitre d' stood, overseeing the waiters with stern attention, snapping his fingers when he saw a table that required service, directing the sommelier to a guest who needed advice as to the proper wine to order with his meal, making certain that each diner felt special.

My waiter, Paul, blond and rosy-cheeked, looked about seventeen years old. He obviously took pleasure in his job. We discussed the menu and when I asked his advice about several of the items listed, he stammered and confessed that, in fact, he had started to work only last week. "My father has been a waiter at this hotel for thirty years and I am following in his footsteps." He glanced with pride at an older man who took care of guests at the other end of the dining room. I placed my order and Paul left, smiling and bowing.

The sommelier brought a glass of wine and I sipped it and observed the other diners—athletic, vibrant with energy, chic in their stylish apres-ski clothes. At that moment, Paul headed down the center of the dining room with the first course for my table and the others surrounding me. He carried the tray high and stole a quick glance toward his father to see if he was observing him in his important mission. As he looked away, he failed to see that the beautiful carpet underneath had buckled. His effort to keep from falling would have done credit to the world's foremost ice skater in the Olympics. But to no avail.

He stumbled, lurched forward and finally fell on his face, soup spilling, dousing everyone within ten feet.

The maitre d' stood over him, his expression severe, motioning for a cleanup crew from the kitchen. Paul, prone on the floor, lifted his face from a soup bowl. Some of the vegetables and cheese had stuck to his hair and eyebrows and chin. His wonderful world had ended! I could have cried for him, and wished I could have interceded with the maitre d' for mercy, but he seemed to be in no mood for interference. He banished

Paul from the dining room with a snap of his fingers and a toss of his head.

I spent the rest of my holiday browsing through the village, making a few purchases from the shopkeepers, walking beside the frozen brook that flowed in warm weather, and visiting the quaint Church of St. Maurice nearby. I walked through the cemetery with its graves of many climbers who had met their deaths in the mountains.

I had brought paperbacks that I had never had time to read at home. How pleasant to sit before the open fire in the main hall of the hotel and read in such a luxurious setting! Time seemed to stand still, the deadlines of my Memphis office unreal and unimportant.

I regretted that I did not see Paul again before I left. The staff at the hotel seemed reluctant to discuss the incident with me, a guest.

Twenty-five years later, in the youth of old age, I went back to Switzerland. I was planning to retire and travel in the United States and realized that this would probably be my last trip to Zermatt. I was anxious to see if it had changed. When I arrived, I was pleasantly surprised. As if held in a delicate suspension of time, it was as charming as I remembered it.

Summer is as lovely as December, but in a different way—wild flowers, rippling streams and clear blue light. An old-fashioned horse–drawn carriage met me when I arrived. The smell of bratwurst and fondue still permeated the air, this time from the sidewalk cafes. We passed the sign directing skiers with broken bones to the proper door. The Matterhorn gleamed as majestically as ever, the invariable warm welcome was extended when I checked into the hotel. Dusk hovered over the village as I unpacked and dressed for dinner. I headed for the dining room, wondering if I would have the same fascination with this generation of guests in their chic clothes and the domineering maitre d' snapping his fingers at his ever obedient waiters.

At the entrance to the elegant dining room, memories washed over me. Burgundy velvet curtains framed the windows, crystal chandeliers sparkled overhead, the same maitre d'—no–no, it couldn't be! It wasn't the same maitre d'—it was Paul!

Amazingly, he remembered me. The thought of looking up into my face from the spilled bowl of soup must have seared my features into his memory. The next day we had a lovely visit over a cup of tea in a small private dining room, and I told him how many times I had thought of him through the years.

"The episode that night seemed to be the end of my dreams," he said. "My father gave me courage, though, when he told me that a similar incident had occurred to him in his youth. And finally, the maitre d' found humor in the situation and decided to give me another chance. I learned not to look up when carrying a tray full of soup and now that I am maitre d', I feel sympathetic towards my young waiters." He smiled, and we sipped our tea in a spirit of friendship and understanding.

I have retired and I often look back on those days of being a "travel consultant." Of the many things I learned throughout my career, the most meaningful was the realization that there are worlds within worlds far more complex than the ones I had pictured before I came to know the people who lived there. I had existed in my own cocoon, my protected bastion, secure from what I perceived to be inconsequential problems in those other worlds.

Why would a falling waiter and a tray of spilled soup in a remote village in Switzerland be of interest to me in my own insulated corner? Because travel opened small windows for me to see inside those other worlds, to become aware of their peoples; their grief became my sorrow, their laughter my joy, and now I share with them in the larger universe that encompasses us all.

THE COMING HOME DRESS

Ruth Crenshaw

I UNTIED the ribbon on the yellowed box and fingered the contents under the blue tissue. While going through the attic trunk, I came across the small box labeled "Andrew's Things." Item by item the memories crowded in: first shoes—once white satin, name bracelet from the hospital, "Quacky," stiff and lifeless, and his Coming Home Dress. Gently I unfolded the tiny cotton garment, trimmed with yellow ribbon and bits of lace gathered at the collar and hem. "Mustn't make it too fancy, or use pink. It may be a boy," I had thought.

Carefully I had sewn joyful anticipation and a prayer into each tiny stitch. I was sure the dress would prove to our baby how much he or she was loved and wanted—no matter that he slept all the way home and never noticed his finery.

How the years have raced by since that day we brought Andrew, our first-born, home. It was a day of days. My mind returns to those months of waiting, the excitement, the suspense—boy or girl? There was no ultra sound in those days to remove the guessing, no clue except predictions from the obstetrician who based them on various signs he had learned from years of experience.

I couldn't take a chance. I had chosen yellow for the baby's things. I even remember how the day was when I gave the old cradle its coat of bright yellow and finished off the pleated skirt at the bottom with a big yellow bow. How silly of me to be so anxious not to show the slightest preference for either a boy or girl! But, it was a boy! Bursting with pride, his father pronounced him perfect. He, being an orthopaedic surgeon, had already examined the baby for dislocated hips or any anatomical imperfections.

In those days children in a hospital were affectionately called "Peter Rabbits." If you were assigned, as a nurse, to pediatrics, you were working on the Peter Rabbit ward. Today the children are called "kids." I often picture little goats running about when I hear the term. So it was, we spoke of our unborn child as the "little rabbit."

Funny how bits of conversations of long ago can come to mind as if it were only yesterday the words were spoken. My due date had passed by two weeks, and the Fourth of July was approaching. My husband said, "Maybe you should aim for Independence Day for the coming out party," as if I were in complete charge of the situation. All that week I had cleaned house: washing windows, cleaning carpets, and rearranging furniture.

"Are you getting your nest ready?" he chided me. "Just like an old mother hen."

Never had I been so full of energy and so happy. But, I must say, when the Fourth came and went, and still no "rabbit," I was disappointed. The next morning I was jarred awake by a kick and the overwhelming sensation that our little one had made the decision that he was ready.

I whispered in my husband's ear, "You had better call the 'delivery man' because 'little rabbit' is about to declare his independence, a day late."

Five days later, Andrew, the little rabbit, was coming home. I had dressed him in the tiny dress I now held in my hands. "How beautiful, this baby," I thought. "But all babies are beautiful." As he was placed in my arms such feelings of joy and reverence engulfed me that I knew my heart would burst. I glanced at my husband and read the same emotions. I noticed, too, that he was driving just a bit more slowly than was his custom. None of his double clutching antics to make me catch my breath and cling to the door so he could get a laugh.

I looked down at the sleeping child and realized I was not the same person I had been when I left home five days ago. I, or we, would never be the same. Even our names were changed forever. We had become father and mother, and were now bound by an unbreakable bond, the miracle of a birth. I had a feeling of awe, of wholeness and completeness. In the hospital I had seen many new mothers and wondered at the glow, the aura, which each seemed to radiate from each one when she held her tiny infant in her arms.

What happens to a woman when she bears a child? I knew the answer now. It was the participation in the miracle of life, the fulfillment and unrestricted love it brings.

I turned to my husband and asked, "Have you ever written a poem?"

"I don't think so. Maybe I wrote sort of one once in the sixth grade which my teacher thought was funny. It was about 'Touch' and 'Roz,'—you know, from 'As You Like It.' Why do you ask?"

"Oh, you wrote about Touchstone and Rosiland," I said. "They say for a man's life to be complete he must write a poem, plant a tree, and have a son. I know you have planted a tree, and I suppose 'Touch' and 'Roz' will count for a poem, and now you have a son. I want your life to be as complete as I feel mine is."

He looked at the baby and me with a smile and said, "Now, what are you going to do with him?"

I answered him with the expression he had often heard at the old Grady Hospital in Atlanta, "I'm gonna try to raise him." We both laughed.

Through the years Andrew's little Coming Home Dress has been packed away with all these other things. The wearing of it marked the beginning of his life with us. I can see his first steps, his first tooth that made me rush to the telephone with the news to his busy father. I hear again his first words and watch his hands at play. How thrilled we were when he started keeping time to music. "He seems to prefer Beethoven," we proudly announced.

Here are his first hard–soled shoes we bought from dear Mr. Whent who worked for Raiford's down on Main Street. Here is the outfit he wore for his first haircut—how sad that day to me. Packed in more tissue is the little satin costume from May Day at Mrs. Hugh's School on Autumn. So serious he was in his role as a page to the princess, the petite pants, cape and banner with the bugle, now lying silent.

Never could I forget his first Christmas with presents under the miniature cedar, aglow with lights. I made him a star for the top from cardboard and tinsel. Now the star, more than a little tarnished, remains the first ornament I hang on the Christmas tree each year.

Events that have filled these passing years flash by: learning to ride a bike, his first erector set, the go-cart, his falling in love with Martha Hopper, his first grade teacher, and then Miss Turner in the second grade—I think partially because she drove a classic Thunderbird, for cars had already become his passion. Near the bottom of the box is a bundle of papers marked "early drawings." They are cars, always cars! Often he was caught filling the margins and flyleaves in his father's important books with his sketches. I have opened those books and found Fords, Buicks, Corvettes and old cars in every blank space.

If I close my eyes, I can hear his drums in the attic and the guitar he was determined to learn to play. His first date remains an etched event. His father drove them to the party at school, but forgot to give him any money. When the punch ran out, he couldn't buy his date a single coke. Never again did we forget to ask, "Do you need any money?"

The day I went up to his room after leaving him at college I knew I had forever left part of me. It's true. Once they fly from the nest they never return as the same offspring who left. He was at another beginning. Everything before had been a rehearsal. Was he ready for the real thing? Now, I was a spectator. I watched from a distance: his college days, his falling in love, their wedding, his graduation from Medical School, and his pride when his son was born. Today his children have brought me back into the circle of his life with a new kind of happiness which all grandmothers cherish.

It's growing dark in the attic as the daylight fades outside. I have been kneeling at the old trunk, living in memory through forty years of Andrew's life. There are boxes for each of our other three children, but for today I have visited with Andrew. I will open the next box tomorrow.

I re-tied the ribbon and replaced the box labeled "Andrew's Things," and closed the trunk. All the days, the eventful times that have made up the years of his life will occupy the special place I hold for him—just as for each of the children. Yet, no other day or time can match that purest joy stitched into the little Coming Home Dress.

POINT IN TIME

Madge Lewis

I should have held the moment close,
Imprisoned and secured,
And brought it out in lonely times
Through which my heart endured.

A sacred talisman, a charm,
To keep our love in trust.
Today the shattered fragments lie
In solitary dust.

MISS BELLE
OF HOOTEN HOLLOW

Anne H. Norris

SOME of the old folks around Hooten Hollow remember when it was just a sleepy little Ozark town, hardly more than a wide place in the road. About the only excitement was on Saturday nights when the young men gathered at Papa Pete's combination cafe and pool hall, as he put it, "to hoot and holler." When the town finally got its own post office, there had been so much talk about "going to hoot and holler," they just made Hooten Hollow the official name. After all, as far as the local folks were concerned, the pronunciation didn't change.

Nowadays the fame of Hooten Hollow is the Ding–a–ling Band, the wonderful trout fishing, and Miss Belle. Actually, Miss Belle should have first billing because without her there would be no Ding–a–lings, nor would trout fishing likely have become such a profitable business.

Miss Belle came to Hooten Hollow as a bride a half century ago, more or less. No one knows her exact age and she has no intention of telling. There is talk among the old–timers, though, that she was a young widow who had vowed never to wed again. Then that handsome Mike Murphy came along and swept her right off her feet and brought her to the town of Hooten Hollow.

It was Mike and Miss Belle who built the first motel in Hooten Hollow and worked up a campaign to attract tourists to the area. It was during the Great Depression of the 1930s. Times were hard for everybody. The local folks had their gardens. What they couldn't grow or buy with the butter-and-egg money, they just had to do without. That is, until the Murphys came to their rescue.

Before they got their motel open, Mike and Miss Belle were off to some of the big cities like Springfield and Little Rock, promoting fall foliage tours, spring flower tours, and summer float fishing in the clear lakes and rivers, and even the beauty and serenity of the winter months in the little valley between the mountains.

They did real well. That is, on all except the winter wonderland stuff. Most people just aren't into getting snowed in somewhere, knowing the roads might be closed for a week or more, no matter how peaceful and pretty it is.

The motel had been open only a few months when Mike Murphy had a fatal heart attack. Most everyone feared Miss Belle would go back to her own family in Illinois, but she proved them wrong. The Murphy Motel had been her Mike's dream, and she intended to see that it was a success.

She worked up a marketing program and a long–range plan long before such things as business forecasting were even thought about. Of course, she didn't know she was doing anything innovative. She was just trying to fill those rooms.

Miss Belle ran ads in all the big city papers within a 500–mile radius of Hooten Hollow, promoting the beauty of the area and the wonderful trout fishing. Her weekend tourist packages included not only rooms at her motel, but also special deals for float fishing, which was beginning to get attention as far away as Chicago. Miss Belle would extol the wonders of floating the clear rivers, with experienced guides who would motor upstream, then keep the boat floating silently back down, allowing those fishing to cast off from the side of the boat. It was virtually guaranteed that everyone who fished would catch his limit, often before noon. Then came the real treat. The guides would dock in a shady cove and before you could say, "The big one got away," the fish fresh out of the lake would be cleaned, cooked in a skillet over a camp fire, and served along with greasy fried potatoes, pork–and–beans, a green salad, and canned peaches for dessert.

There was one thing that bothered Miss Belle when she bragged about the wonders of float fishing. She never had personally had such an experience. When her cousin Betty came for a visit, they decided the time had come. They were going float fishing.

Back then float fishing down the Buffalo and White Rivers was a sport that excluded women for the most part. Although Miss Belle was not aware of it at the time, when she called Bowe's Boat Dock to set up their float trip, none of the guides wanted the job. The fact is, they drew straws to see who would have to take the two ladies.

All the fellows were waiting at the dock the next morning to see if the ladies showed up. If they hadn't had so much respect for Miss Belle and weren't indebted to her for most of their float business, there probably would have been some real belly-laughing when those ladies stepped out of the car. Cousin Betty had on blue jeans and a plaid shirt, but this kind of outfit wasn't in Miss Belle's wardrobe.

Miss Belle was always the proper lady. For one thing, she wouldn't think of leaving home without wearing a girdle. So under that pretty blue one-piece jumpsuit, she was properly girdled down. Her blonde hair was stylishly pushed back under a flower–bedecked straw hat, and her leather ankle boots matched the tan and yellow scarf that protruded from her shirt pocket. She was ready for the big day on the river.

Actually, just as Miss Belle always said, fishing was good. Under the direction of the guide, who baited their hooks, showed them how to cast, and then took off the fish and rebaited for them, the ladies did real well. In fact, when all the boats docked for lunch, the men were beginning to show a little respect for the two, albeit reluctantly.

It was while the guides were cooking the fish and getting lunch ready that Miss Belle realized a one–piece jumpsuit isn't the appropriate attire for float fishing. "Over the hill and far away" is about the best way to describe toilet facilities along the river bank. The men took off to the left and the two ladies climbed a hill over to the right. The only way to describe what happened next is to say that with the one-piece jumpsuit and the tight girdle down around her ankles, Miss Belle sort of got overbalanced and down the hill she went, in a squatting position and waddling like a duck.

What followed depends on whose version you hear. But Miss Belle was a good sport. She bought some blue jeans, saved the jumpsuit for shopping trips, and threw away the girdle!

Although the Murphy Motel did well during fishing season, Miss Belle needed year-round business. That's how the Ding–a–lings got started. Hooten Hollow had become a Mecca for retirees. Miss Belle decided to organize a senior citizens' band. It was a success from the start, beyond her wildest dreams. They were quite appropriately called the "Ding–a–lings." Some of the band members actually could play real instruments, such as the fiddle, banjo, flute, and keyboard. Others played cow bells, spoons, wash boards, combs, sticks tapped together—whatever they found to serve the purpose. They practiced at the Murphy Motel and often stayed for lunch or dinner. Many returned on Sunday for the noon buffet.

Miss Belle turned her seldom–used meeting room into a supper club. On Friday and Saturday nights the local folks came to eat and dance. Special entertainment was furnished by the Ding–a–lings. It might seem unbelievable, but they were good! They even received an invitation to play at one of the parties in Washington during the President's inauguration.

The thrill of the invitation was dimmed by the realization that there would be considerable expense involved. A bus would have to be chartered to get them there. Rooms in Washington would be very expensive. And, even oldies like to eat.

Once again, it was Miss Belle to the rescue!

She began planning a money–raising Thanksgiving dance, with all proceeds going toward the Ding–a–lings' Washington trip. Ads were run in daily and weekly papers for miles around. Posters went up in store windows. A banner stretched across the front of the courthouse. Band members sold advance tickets and sought cash donations and pledges from local businesses. Excitement spread like wildfire.

A special feature for the event was to be a dance contest. This, of course, was another of Miss Belle's ideas. She promised a Thanksgiving turkey to the winning couple.

The big night finally came. A crowd soon filled the motel's former meeting room, decorated with crepe paper streamers and cutout turkeys.

The dance contest commenced. Competition was fierce, but the final decision of the judges went to a young couple who jitter–bugged their way to the top. They would be the recipients of Miss Belle's Thanksgiving turkey, and they waited on the stage with the band, receiving the judges' congratulations, while Miss Belle went to get their prize.

The couple's expectation of a turkey that would be thawed and roasted for their Thanksgiving dinner left with the reentrance of Miss Belle, not carrying a frozen turkey but leading a real, live gobbler. She held a long red ribbon attached to a little band around the turkey's neck. He followed along quite nicely—until the crowd realized what was happening. They clapped and cheered and stomped their feet.

The surprise of the winning couple was nothing compared to that of the turkey. Terrified by all the noise, he broke loose from Miss Belle's leash and took off flying around the room, squawking and flapping his wings. Feathers were falling, and that wasn't all! The people tried to cover their heads with their hands as they ran out of the room.

After the turkey finally was caught, the tables and chairs wiped clean, and the floor swept and mopped, the folks came back in and the party resumed.

Poor Miss Belle! She kept saying, "But I practiced walking in with the turkey and he did just great." She just hadn't considered the action of the crowd and the reaction of the turkey!

All in all, the evening was a success. Enough money was raised to send the Ding–a–lings to Washington. The turkey lived happily ever after at a neighbor's farm because the winning couple refused to accept him. Best of all, Miss Belle celebrated Thanksgiving with a full house at the Murphy Motel.

MORTIMER THE MOUSE

Ethel Joyner

HE WAS no ordinary mouse. He did not share the love for the great outdoors with his family of field mice. Mortimer was an inside kind of mouse. He preferred the Hortons' house where there were always roaring fires in the fireplace in the winter, and a cool–air retreat in the hot summer weather.

He felt great concern for his family in their ongoing struggle to survive in the outside world. They were constantly scurrying about to find a haven from the harsh elements and protection from the farm cats.

A feeling of warmth and security enveloped Mortimer each time he entered his secret place—a tiny opening in the baseboard of Mrs. Mary Horton's sitting room. He had remained undetected for many months, but one evening Mrs. Horton spotted him crouched in a dark corner of the room. Her bloodcurdling screams brought in the whole family who found her, pale and shaken, standing on top of a table. Mortimer heard

Tom Horton say he had made the decision to bring in Tabby, the cat, who was certain to nab the culprit in short order. He also said that for backup security, mousetraps would be placed in strategic places throughout the house. Mortimer realized that Mr. Horton was determined that his wife would never again have the wits scared out of her by such "a brazen little rodent."

Mortimer, tucked far back in the secret opening, felt his skin prickle as he listened to all these elaborate plans for his extermination. He decided that it would be wise to avoid the house, especially while Tabby was on patrol, but he was amused at the idea that the Hortons thought he would fall for the mousetrap ploy. One of the primary rules stressed in his survival training was how to avoid traps, no matter how tempting the cheese.

After a time of staying undercover, Mortimer could not resist a strong urge to revisit the secret place. He noted that Tabby was once again an outside cat, and quickly spotted the trap in the corner loaded with cheese. Tiptoeing cautiously around the trap, he remembered the horror stories his family had handed down to the younger generation about the relatives who had come to a swift and terrible end while innocently nibbling away at the deadly morsels. Mortimer's survival training and innate intelligence had served him well. He congratulated himself on being observant and clever and a most extraordinary mouse.

That night, re–entering the opening, he found Mary Horton busily engaged at her computer. Observing her, he was filled with a yearning to be a part of the Horton family. There was Tabby the Cat, Wanda the Fish, Sparky the Dog, so why not him—Mortimer the Mouse? It sounded so logical. He was certain that he would become the favorite household pet, once they got to know him.

Mortimer watched in fascination as Mary Horton operated the computer, her hand over an object that seemed to control the action on the screen. It was really amazing how those things worked and he wondered what the object was that she moved around with her hand. He was startled when she suddenly threw both hands up in the air. In exasperation she said, "My goodness, this mouse has quit working. I must call the repairman."

Mortimer's ears perked up as he thought over Mary Horton's remark. "So that's what it is—a mouse! A non-working mouse!" She had opened the door with that statement. "Maybe I could take his place," he mused. "I would work hard, and they will see what a valuable addition I would be to their household."

He visualized Mary Horton's hand covering his tiny body, moving him around on the table which, in turn, would produce images on the computer screen. He could hardly contain his excitement.

Mortimer waited until the next morning and carefully made his way into the sitting room. Skirting the mousetrap, he made his way up the table and positioned himself on top of the computer where he sat patiently awaiting Mary Horton's return to her computer with the non-working mouse. In a short time, she came into the room with the repairman. On spying Mortimer she screamed in horror, throwing herself into the arms of the astonished repairman.

She sobbed, "He's back—the mouse!"

The uproar brought in the entire household. Tabby skulked around the room, Sparky barked, and Wanda gurgled in her fishbowl, but Mortimer, sensing imminent danger, had long since abandoned the premises.

Outside with his family, he told of his adventure and his desire to be an inside mouse and to belong to the Horton family. He was disillusioned as he pondered his destiny.

Although his psyche was wounded, his self-esteem at an all time low, Mortimer reflected on the rewarding aspects of his life: a warm and loving support group—dozens of sisters, brothers and cousins, his mom and dad, and the vast outdoors where action was plentiful for an adventurous mouse. And he could always return to the secret place to observe if the non-working computer mouse had decided to re-enter the work force.

FATHER MURPHY'S HAT

Madge H. Lewis

SEAN O'LEARY'S true Irish tenor rang through the streets of New York City's lower east side, filling the air with the words that had been chanted by his young friends at recess on the school playground.

> *"Father Murphy lost his hat*
> *Some say this and some say that*
> *Most folks say that it is at*
> *Widow Mulrooney's cozy flat."*

Doors and windows flew open with a clatter as shocked faces peered out of the tenement houses that marked his route. The disgraceful words hung in the air, charging the crisp sunlit afternoon with an atmosphere of stunned disbelief.

Sean gave no thought to his unexpected audience as he skipped along at an energetic pace, his cheeks pink with excitement and the joy of turning ten years old this very day in the year of Our Lord 1890. He was fresh from the old sod, just getting used to the strange ways of Americans. But of two things he was certain: he could beat up every boy in the block, even the older, bigger ones and he could sing better at Sunday Mass than any of Father Murphy's "little angels" in the choir.

He continued his song right up to the door of the basement apartment where they lived and Sean was startled out of his wits when his mother grabbed him by the collar as he entered, her face distorted with anger.

"Sean O'Leary, whatever do ye think ye be doing, singing like that about our sainted Father Murphy? Just ye wait till I give yer father an earful when he comes home from a hard day's work." She boxed his ears and stood back with a disapproving look.

"Sure and it's true, Mam," Sean said, grimacing, worried for a bit that this time he'd gone over the top. "All the lads at school were talkin' about it and I seen him meself on the way home from school. He was comin' outta the Widow Mulrooney's door and she be standin' there, all dressed up and wavin' goodbye to him. He had his hat on then so perhaps he'd gone back to fetch it. He was smilin' and happy, like he might be..."

"Might be what, Sean O'Leary?" She wiped her hands on her apron and continued to glare at him

"Well, Mam, he was lookin' like he might be smitten with her." Sean dodged her whack and escaped through the door and up the small narrow steps to the tiny storage area that his Da had converted into a sleeping room. His Mam couldn't follow him there—the stairs were too steep. He stopped at the top of the stairway and held his hand over his mouth so she wouldn't see him laugh. She was short and round, and her naturally ruddy complexion turned even redder as she tried to hoist herself up the stairs after him.

"Don't try to make it up the steps, Mam. I'll sing ye the song from up here."

He settled himself on the small cot that served as his bed and once again his voice rang out, "Father Murphy lost his hat, some say this and some say that—what do ye say, Mam?"

"Sean O'Leary, don't ye be forgettin' ye'll be goin' to confession to Father Murphy tomorrow afternoon. Are ye goin' to confess to him that ye spread lies and tales about him and the Widow Mulrooney?" Mrs. O'Leary gave up on her efforts to climb the stairs. She was too wide and they were too narrow.

"Well, Mam, I 'spose I'll confess that I know a secret about a priest and a pretty young widder lady. I'll ask him 'What should I be doin' with this information that's come me way, Father Murphy?' He'll tell me what to do and ye can't hold it against me if I do me penance the way he tells me to—now, can ye, Mam?"

"Ye don't know anything, Sean O'Leary. Ye made it all up and we'll wait till yer father gets home. He'll most likely take the switch to ye. Then we'll see how ye can really sing!"

Sean heard her muttering about him as she went into the tiny kitchen to begin the night meal she always had waiting for Da when he got in from a hard day's work. Her grumbling always faded into praise when she discussed him with others or even with Sean himself. With her squeezing and hugging, she'd say his name meant "Gift from God." Then she would tell him how handsome he was with his blue eyes and his dark curly hair and the roses of Killarney in his cheeks. He was getting too big for daft talk like that and he lived in fear that she would shame him in front of some of the lads from school.

The smell of meat pasties and bread baking wafted up the stairs and Sean's mouth watered at the thought of his mother's fine cooking. He could hardly wait for Da to come home so they could eat. But suppose his Mam and Da made him go to bed without his supper? Sean's stomach growled at the thought of it. He'd probably waste away during the night and be dead in the light of the morning.

He shouldn't have teased his Mam that way. She didn't take kindly to anything said against her sainted Father Murphy. 'Twas true Father Murphy had taken them in on their day of arrival three months ago and helped them find this place to live. Then he had gone with Sean's father to the Kehoe Iron Works and put in a good word with old Patrick Kehoe. That was how Connor O'Leary got his first job in America, how they had been able to put food on their table from the very beginning. Though they were poor like the other newly arrived Irish, all the good things that had happened had been because of Father Murphy.

Sean lay back on the cot and stared at the low ceiling. He was as grateful as a ten year old boy could be but the ditty that had first been bandied about the school playground continued to play its addictive tune over and over in his head. He wondered why everyone was taking such a turn over Father Murphy leaving his hat at Widow Mulrooney's flat. He couldn't understand the strange goings–on of grown–ups.

When Connor O'Leary got home from work, there was hardly room for anything or anyone else in their tiny quarters. He dwarfed everything around him, like a sturdy oak surrounded by fragile saplings. Sean peeked down the stairway and saw him grab his Mam and give her a big kiss. "No one knows how to kiss like an Irishman," Connor often said, along with other comments of pride about his countrymen. "Those Dirty British could learn a thing or two from the likes of us Irish," he bragged. Sean always had thought that Dirty British was the only way an Englishman could be described until he started to school. Sister Ermanelda punished him five times before he finally learned to say just "British," and he used his father's descriptive words only when he was out of earshot of the nuns.

Sean crept to the top of the stairway so he could hear the whispered conversation between his Mam and his Da. He knew his Mam was telling Da all about the song and about Father Murphy's hat. Sean's heart eased a bit when he heard his father's reply, "Sure, and I'll let it pass for this night, being as it's his birthday. I'll have a good talk with the lad tomorrow."

Sean could hear the sound of his father opening a pint and settling back in his big comfortable chair, which had been given to them by Father Murphy. "I fancy a good meal tonight, me darlin'. Be sure to make up some of those fine potato cakes you're so good at. And how about sticky buns for dessert?" Sean was glad that his father was a jovial man when he was on the dry, but even more cheery after several pints. They had a good life, he and Mam and Da.

"I planned to ask you to paddle him good and let him go to bed hungry," his mother was saying, "I'm worried about him singin' that silly ditty on the way home from school. His voice carries like a town crier. The whole neighborhood will likely be talkin' about poor Father Murphy." She poured some of the next pint into a glass for herself. She liked a nip or two while she was cooking. "I have a fine meal bakin' in the oven for ye," she said as she sifted flour into the already cooked potatoes and began to shape them into cakes just the way Connor liked them.

When Sean was finally called downstairs for his supper, his heart was pounding in his chest. He hoped his Mam didn't prod Da into havin' his talk with him tonight. Still, he was too much like his Da to show fear, so he bounded down the steps and into the room with his usual boisterous air.

"Happy Birthday, boy–o," Connor said, throwing an arm around him. "Ten years old today, eh? Well, your Mam and I have a little parcel here for ye to open to help ye celebrate the big occasion. Will ye be openin' it now?"

"Sure, Da. Thanks, Mam." He stooped down to give his short little mother a kiss. The day was not far off when he could pick her up like his Da. He would get many a good laugh in the future when she chastised him and tried to punish him—ah, she would have a merry time of it staying ahead of himself.

Sean sat down cross–legged in the middle of the floor and began to open his birthday gift. He was heartened that his parents were going to let the Father Murphy incident go unnoticed, at least for his birthday night. When he had removed the wrapping paper from the parcel and saw the baseball glove, he squealed with delight. It was just what he had wanted ever since he had learned that all Americans were crazy about baseball, just like the British were about cricket.

"I thought I could throw ye a few pitches behind the house when the days are long enough for us to be outside in the evenings," his father reached over and gave him an affectionate jab on his jaw.

"Thanks, Da. I'll take it to school and we can get in a good game at recess. Father Murphy has a fancy for the game, too, and maybe he'll..." Sean stopped suddenly as his Mam gave him a chastening look and his Da gazed unhappily at the floor.

Sean ran upstairs to get his ball, more to relieve the tension than to play with his mitt. When he returned they all sat down at the rough table to say the blessing and partake of the fine birthday meal for this very special occasion.

On the next day, Saturday, little work was done by the ladies of the Irish community. Sean saw his Mam gossiping over the fence. He went with her to the green grocer's on the trolley and couldn't help but hear the serious talk on the subject that seemed the center of everyone's thoughts.

Mrs. Mullins said in a half-whisper, "I always thought there was somethin' just a bit too goody–goody about that widow woman."

Old Mrs. Cole who spent half her days on her knees in church spoke solemnly, "We must all say a novena. I pray to the saints above that our dear Father Murphy will come back to his senses before too long."

The lads and lassies went to confession at the regular time in the afternoon, and they all looked frightened and ashamed as they knelt in the pews awaiting their turn. Sean felt certain he would receive a severe penance as he was the guilty one who had spread the news by singing the now infamous ditty throughout the lower east side.

When his turn came, he entered the confessional, fell to his knees and in a trembling voice, said, "Bless me, Father, for I have sinned." He choked and felt such remorse he was hardly able to continue. But sure and St. Patrick must have laid his hand on Sean's shoulder for he blurted out the whole sordid story and then was ashamed that a few tears trickled down his cheeks. Father Murphy charged him to think before he spoke and to beware of idle gossip. Sean could not believe it was over. He only knew that he was free to go and that he had been given a penance of three Our Fathers and three Hail Marys. In fact, that's what all the lads got except Benny Cole who always had a long list of sins to confess. He usually had to say a whole rosary.

Even Da was not as harsh in his punishment as Sean had expected. "You must learn to respect your elders, boy-o," his father told him sternly when he came home from work. "Especially the priest of the parish. Suppose you go to bed without your supper tonight and promise that you'll never say an unkind word again about the good father."

Sean breathed a sigh of relief. He didn't mind missing his supper. He had sneaked a big sticky bun up to his room last night—just in case.

Much later Sean positioned himself once again in his perch to listen to Da as he described to Mam the evening he had just spent at Bycie Mullins' neighborhood pub. Da was a fine story teller and Sean could picture the men crowded around as Bycie held court. Listening to Da he almost felt as though he had been there.

"Tis a fine kettle of fish, this business," Bycie had said, shaking his reddish brown head. "Niver did I think I'd be hearin' an unkind word against the good father. But 'tis serious business, my friends, serious business, indeed." He had filled the tin cups all around and the drinking and talking went on far into the wee hours. Many an Irish tale was recounted, prayers were promised for poor Father Murphy in his weakness, old proverbs were quoted that hadn't been thought of in America since their little community had settled in this part of New York City. It was a profitable night for Bycie Mullins. Da said there had never been an evening quite like it.

Sunday morning every pew in church was filled, and chairs had to be brought in for the overflow. Everyone knelt in silent prayer and Sean sensed they were asking the God Almighty above to forgive Father Murphy, to have him repent for his waywardness, but Sean was filled with wonder that leaving a hat at Widow Mulrooney's could be such a big sin.

He was sure that they also sent upwards a grudging request for the saving of the soul of the sinful Widow Mulrooney as the entire congregation watched her enter the church and settle gracefully into her pew. She dressed a little too fine to suit the ladies of St. Christopher's. She had auburn hair and sparkling green eyes, and Sean thought she looked real pert for a lady almost thirty years old.

The candles on the altar were lit and Father Murphy came out with the altar boys all crisp and neat in their cassocks and surplices and began the beautiful Latin mass. His white hair and ruddy cheeks presented a colorful sight against the splendor of the elegant green vestments and the gold of the tabernacle.

When Father Murphy climbed the stairs to the pulpit, hardly a sound could be heard. No one coughed or sneezed, no babies cried, and even old Mrs. Callahan ceased her snoring.

Father Murphy looked out upon his flock with his angelic smile, showering his love on each and every one of them. There was a halo of a laugh about the priest, something joyous and forgiving.

"Surely he can't be knowin' about all the gossip that's been bandied around. He wouldna' look like that," whispered Da as he reached over to take hold of his wife's plump little hand.

"My dear parishioners, what a happy day this is for all of us. God has seen fit to make the sun shine and the birds sing today. 'Tis a spring day to remember—in more ways than one—and here I am this Sunday morning, the bearer of news."

Bycie Mullins sat up straight in his pew although it must have been hard for him to keep his eyes open after the late closing of his pub. Bennie Cole quit fidgeting and actually listened to Father Murphy. Patrick Kehoe looked questioningly at his tiny little wife, whose face was equally puzzled. Sean O'Leary took hold of his father's other hand and they sat in the pew, a picture of solidarity, curious, wondering, ever hopeful that Father Murphy was not going to tell them that he was leaving the priesthood, that he and the Widow Mulrooney would be going elsewhere. A tear rolled down Sean's cheeks as he thought of how different their lives would be without Father Murphy.

"As you all know well, we Irish are dreamers of dreams. I have for many years consulted with our good bishop to assist our little parish in an endeavor that is dear to my heart. There is a fine summer camp just six hours away from us by rail and His Excellency has told me that this year the diocese would contribute two weeks of summer camp for the lads of our parish in the month of June and the same for the young lasses in July. Now, you can see, I was presented with quite a problem there—where to get the cost of the train fare. So, after praying and asking the Almighty Lord to give me some sign, I received a note from one of our faithful parishioners, Mrs. Seamus Mulrooney. She asked me to call on her to discuss an important matter."

The congregation began to stir. Mrs. Callahan's soft snore started up again, but was hurriedly quieted by Mary Flanagan who sat beside her. Bennie Cole began to squirm in his seat and received a discreet tap on his kneecap from his mother.

"Mrs. Mulrooney advised me that she had been left a sum of money by a dear aunt who just recently passed away. It was her wish to share it with the parish. She has generously offered to pay the railroad fare for each child old enough to attend the camp. The lads and lassies will have a fine chance to enjoy the fresh air and the swimming in the lake at Camp Marymount. Mrs. Mulrooney will welcome you to her home to sign up your children for this wonderful experience."

As shame and humiliation swept through the congregation, Father Murphy descended the steps of the pulpit and made his way back to the altar. Heads were bowed. They fell to their knees as though on cue. The benediction that followed Mass was more beautiful than ever; the sun had surely shone down upon the poor people of the parish of St. Christopher's. When the congregation all joined in to sing the closing hymn, "Holy God, We Praise Thy Name," Sean O'Leary's Irish tenor rang clear and true above all the other voices.

On June lst, Sean and his fellow students, along with their families and Father Murphy, clustered together at the rail station. Suddenly it was there alongside, the big black locomotive, huge and screaming, the whistle sounding in heavy blasts with cinders and smoke pouring out, impelling the excited group to pull back and protect their eyes. Finally it came to a full stop, and amidst much clamor and confusion the boys clambered aboard the waiting train, with Sean yelling taunts at the girls that they'd have a thing or two to tell them when they got back.

Handkerchiefs fluttered from the women's hands, some shedding a tear or two for the missing of a son for the next two weeks. Sean waved goodbye to his Mam and Da and to the Widow Mulrooney who was there to give them her good wishes for a grand trip.

Just as the train gave a great heave and started on its journey a gust of wind blew Father Murphy's hat off his head. It skittered down the tracks after the train, twisting and turning, then was picked up by an errant breeze and carried away. All eyes were on the disappearing hat, which sometimes rose with the wind into the air, sometimes dipping down again to speed its way along the tracks. Sean O'Leary leaned precariously out the window of the train and the breeze picked up the words that he sang out and carried them back to the waving, laughing crowd:

"Sure and begorrah, any man can lose his hat in a fairy–wind."

THE PHANTOM AND THE GHOST

Ethel Joyner

THE LONG–AWAITED news finally arrived. The theatre had landed the widely acclaimed production of *The Phantom of the Opera*. It was cause for celebration by a weary board beset with mounting debt and dismal prospects for the future of their beloved theatre.

A week before the opening of the show, jubilant board members were advised that advance box office revenue had exceeded expectations and they were clear of debt. The lights would not be dimmed on the marquee of the majestic old theatre as they had feared!

Shortly after the arrival of the Broadway troupe, preparations for opening night were begun. The theatre was a bustling hub of activity as the cast began rehearsal with the crew working around the clock to ready the stage. Everything went according to script: the chandelier fell from the ceiling on cue, and the massive old organ responded to the phantom's urging with thunderous,

169

mournful chords portending the tragic events that were to unfold in the play.

Watching from the balcony was a young girl dressed in an old-fashioned white lace dress. Her black hair hung in braids over her shoulders. Her face was pale and her dark eyes angry as she observed the activity on the stage. The actors and crew were unaware of her presence because she was invisible. Her name was Mary. She was a ghost, and her spirit had taken up residence in the old theatre. Startled theater–goers often swore they had seen her seated alone in the curtained loge, her slight body bathed in a soft ethereal glow. On occasion, brave–hearted spectators would venture into the loge only to see her vanish into the air before their eyes.

The little ghost was happiest when the theatre was dark and she could play the organ to her heart's content. In the early morning hours many a stagehand, in the process of dismantling the stage, was seen hurriedly leaving the theatre, white and shaken, as the organ, unaccompanied, began to peal soul–stirring hymns of old.

Throughout the years of being resident ghost, Mary had not experienced an incident that posed a threat or caused her alarm, but the phantom, a fellow–ghost who had disrupted an opera, was clearly an evil force, casting shadows of doubt and insecurity on her otherwise happy and peaceful existence.

"He must be stopped," she vowed as she devised a plan that would put an end to the intrusive phantom.

Opening night was a disaster. The chandelier swayed dangerously, and the theatre patrons gasped in horror as it appeared to plunge in their midst before stopping precariously overhead. A dissonant version of Rock of Ages swelled from the organ at the hands of a bewildered phantom. The lighting was alternately blindingly white or pitch black. The props shifted mysteriously, gliding off stage as the terrified actors ran into the wings. The theatre closed the second night of the run as management assured the patrons that it would reopen after certain "repairs and adjustments" were made.

The producers of the show gathered hurriedly to determine the cause of the opening night disaster and how they could salvage the show. Upon learning the theatre was inhabited by a ghost, they concluded that the ghost had wrought the destruction because of fear and jealousy created by the phantom's presence. It was decided the survival of the show would depend on the phantom's convincing the ghost that he posed no threat to her.

In the early morning hours in the darkened theatre, he strode onto the stage. Directing his plea to the invisible ghost seated in the loge, he spoke.

"I plead with you for the life of this show, for I am no threat to you. I am a writer's creation, a make–believe phantom, an actor behind a mask." Stripping the mask from his face, bowing deeply, he continued, "Mary, you are the spirit of this grand old theatre. No other shall take your place, and you shall so remain forevermore!"

The phantom's eloquent plea convinced Mary that she would always be the resident ghost, and her fears disappeared. She became an ardent fan of the phantom. The play broke all box office records, and for the first time in its history, the theatre reported excellent profits.

Theatre patrons were unaware of the invisible little girl who nightly joined the phantom as, side by side, they played magical music together on the mighty pipe organ.

LEAH'S LAMENT

Ethel Joyner

I am not a great beauty, easy to see,
But, Lord, stop Jacob from looking at Rachel.
      Let him look at me!

God, how sad it was that you allowed
Rachel to be so lovely, so well–endowed.
God, forgive me, it seems so unfair
That I was not bequeathed an equal share.
She with fair skin and long raven tresses,
With his eyes he admires, adores, caresses.

I am not a great beauty, easy to see,
But, Lord, stop Jacob from looking at Rachel.
      Let him look at me!

I am Laban's first born, I have first choice.
Rachel, the second born, should have no voice.
There will be others who travel from Canaan's Land
To woo my sister, to seek her hand.
Lord, justice would be served, don't you suppose,
If Rachel could grow a wart on the end of her nose?

I am not a great beauty, easy to see,
But, Lord, stop Jacob from looking at Rachel.
Let him look at me!

THE DENIAL OF SUE ANN

Rita Bernero West

Sue Ann was her name, she set hearts aflame,
And was by one and all admired.
She was a Southern belle (to a fare-thee-well),
In her youth she was much desired.

Sue finally chose from one of her beaux,
Wed a man with money connections.
Her life was all play; there was bridge every day,
With snacks and dainty confections.

Club dinners were fine, not to mention the wine,
Then Sue saw a change in her size.
Ah, but no one wore a silly size four,
And Sue hardly blinked her eyes

As the years went by, Sue failed to try
To curb her great appetite.
She cheered, "This is yummy!" and sucked in her tummy,
Always the bright socialite

Sue discovered one day to her grim dismay,
She appeared to have got plump.
An inch or so here, it was painfully clear,
And way too much in the rump.

Calories, she supposed, were the cause of her woes,
So Sue decided to count.
But the right number of these left her not very pleased,
And she sneaked in a greater amount.

A friend's remark, one day in the park,
"Carbohydrates are not for you,"
Set Sue to worrying and sent her scurrying
To check this new ballyhoo.

At first it was easy; everything was so greasy,
But starches were her Waterloo.
Oh, what could be done when you weighed a ton?
"I must find a way," cried Sue

Aerobics were out; she wasn't that stout
And jogging would mess up her hair.
"Count fat grams instead," is what they all said.
That, too, was a dismal affair

Cellulite was a word she should never had heard,
But the mirror was telling the truth.
Liposuction was there, if she'd care to dare,
But Sue was too long in the tooth

So she thought after all, though I may not be small,
My money and status are admired.
I'm a real Southern belle (to a fare-thee-well),
So surely I'm still much desired.

WHERE'S MR. PURDY?

Anne H. Norris

JUST the mention of Mr. Purdy sends my friend Julius and me into fits of laughter. We've actually never met Mr. Purdy. But he almost broke up our budding romance.

Julius had come to the city where I live for a business conference. We had been introduced by a mutual friend who knew we had a lot of common interests. For one thing, we were both single parents with teenage children. The trials and tribulations of parenthood gave us plenty to talk about during the evening, which included a wonderful Italian dinner with several bottles of red wine. We parted at the airport, looking forward to his return in six weeks.

Julius phoned me at least once a day, and I would rush home from my office to see what kind of mail I might have received. Daily cards reflected his great sense of humor. The florist truck was seen in my driveway so often, neighbors thought I was having an affair with the delivery man. I think we both had been bitten by the love bug.

My excitement mounted as the day drew near for Julius to return. I had planned to meet him at the airport, and I was a bit apprehensive. After all, it had been six weeks since our one evening together. Would he be as wonderful as I remembered? Maybe I wouldn't recognize him!

The big day finally came. I was up at the crack of dawn. I changed clothes at least six times before settling on what to wear. The new outfit I had bought for the occasion did seem a bit dressy for going to the airport. I decided to save that red silk for the next evening. The blue suit would be more appropriate. Julius liked blue. I was wearing a blue dress when we met, and he said it was a perfect match for my eyes.

This being such a special occasion, I thought I should have my hair done so I made a three o'clock appointment at the beauty shop. Julius' plane wasn't due in until 5:50. I knew I would have plenty of time. Wrong! First off, his plane made a brief stop in Chicago and he dashed off to give me a quick call at the office. The receptionist told him I had gone to the beauty shop. She went on to tell him that I wouldn't be back in the office that afternoon because I was going to meet someone at the airport.

If the manicurist hadn't insisted that I should have my nails done, I wouldn't have been late getting to the airport. I had planned it all so carefully. I would be at the gate waiting. But the plane got there before I did. When I first saw Julius, he was walking down the corridor toward me with an attentive lady at his side. Seeing that they were engaged in conversation, it was obvious to me that they were acquainted. My first thought was that they had been seated next to each other on the plane and would part company when I reached them. Wrong again! When she realized that I was about to extend a welcome to Julius, she actually grabbed his arm. I couldn't believe what I was seeing. I gave Julius a very cool peck on his cheek and waited for an introduction—or an explanation. I got neither.

With Julius in the middle, the three of us walked to the baggage area. Nothing was said until Julius asked me to hold his brief case while he retrieved his bags. That female acquaintance of his (whoever she was!) tried to jerk it right out of my hand. "I will hold that for him," she said. Not on your life, I thought. I yanked it back and told her in no uncertain terms that I would hold the brief case.

Once outside the terminal, I very coolly advised that my car was parked in lane C. "That woman" said emphatically that *her* car was in lane B. Julius just stood there, looking from her to me. "You handle this any way you want to," I said to him, "I'm going to my car." As I opened my car door, I looked back and could see they were still right where I had left them. But I couldn't hear what was being said. Julius turned and headed my way. When he could stop laughing, he explained what had happened.

When he had arrived, he looked for me. Of course I wasn't there since I was late. The mystery lady walked up as if she were expecting him. Right off, he figured she was someone from my office. After all, when he called from Chicago, my overly–efficient receptionist had told him I had gone to the beauty shop. It made sense to him that I had sent one of the secretaries to meet him. He was puzzled, though, when we met in the corridor just a few minutes later and I didn't introduce them. Also, he couldn't understand why he got such a cool reception.

The conversation in the parking lot cleared it up. The lady had been sent to the airport to meet a Mr. Purdy, who was to be the speaker that evening at a convention dinner. Although she had never met Mr. Purdy, the description she had been given fit Julius, and it was obvious he was looking around as though expecting someone to meet him.

One thing had upset the lady. She was shocked that he had a girlfriend, a mistress, or whatever. Even worse, this hussy had the nerve to come to the airport to meet him! Nevertheless, she had been sent to meet Mr. Purdy and take him to the hotel. She intended to do just that.

As Julius and I were putting his bags in my car, we looked back. There she stood, in total disbelief that she had failed her assignment. Tears ran down her cheeks as she wailed, "But where's Mr. Purdy?"

WHEN AUGUST TERRY HELD COURT

Nelle Weddington

WHEN Mr. August Terry lived in the house on the corner of our street in Hattiesburg, there was always something going on.

Mr. Terry, whom we sometimes called Mr. August, or plain Mr. T., was a Justice of the Peace, better known as a JP. JPs were local judges who performed important and varied civil duties.

Not everybody was as lucky as we were. Just by sitting on our own front porch and watching up the street, we could see a better show in one afternoon than some of the things prime–time television offers right now.

For example, on any given day a policeman might pull up to the door at Mr. Terry's house bringing in some well–known citizen who couldn't hold his liquor. Leaning on the strong arm of the law, the sodden creature would stagger up Mr. T.'s steps, and there on

181

the porch, Mr. T. would hold court. If you were listening closely, you might even learn what the fine would be.

We never knew who'd be next. Folks were brought in for all sorts of misdemeanors, from some wild jayhawks racing around town all the way to a bloody fist fight at Uncle Bob's Place down under the hill. Fair and square, Mr. T. meted out justice.

The people we really enjoyed, however, were most likely to arrive on Saturday or Sunday afternoon. A car or two would pull up at Mr. Terry's house. The man, who usually looked more like a boy, would jump out and stride hurriedly up to the door. After a brief conversation with Mr. Terry, the young fellow would rush back to the car, swing open the door, and out would hop the cutest, prettiest girl you ever saw, all dressed up, giggling, and holding the boy's arm tighter than a June bug on a ripe blackberry.

Maybe they'd step inside for the wedding ceremony, but sometimes it was held on the porch.

When the ceremony was over, Mr. Terry always collected his fee—and kissed the bride!

There was one event in Mr. Terry's late years which none of us will ever forget. It happened after Mrs. Terry had died, the children were grown and gone, and things were real quiet on our street.

One night about nine o'clock we heard sirens blowing and saw flashing blue lights at Mr. Terry's. Police and ambulance attendants raced up the walk. They beat on the front door, got no response, and rushed to the back. Still no answer. By that time the neighbors had gathered. Voices got higher and more excited.

Then, one big fellow put his shoulder to the old door and pushed. The door gave way. In rushed the man with police and ambulance attendants at his heels. In less than a minute the attendants ran back to the ambulance, pulled out the stretcher, returned to the house, and in no time at all here they came again, this time bearing the prostrate figure of Mr. Terry.

We watched as they loaded him into the ambulance. Doors banged shut. Sirens blared. Blue lights flashed, and Mr. T. was on his way to the hospital.

However, early the next morning, to our delighted surprise, Mr. Terry was seen sitting in his rocker on his own front porch taking in the warm sunshine. We were relieved, of course, but this dramatic recovery presented more mystery than the neighbors could handle.

During the day, bit by bit—as neighbors drifted by—the story unfolded. It developed that on the previous evening, Mr. T. had been engaged in a rather lengthy telephone conversation with the current lady of his affections (who she was we never knew). As she talked on and on in her sweet, melodious voice, and Mr. Terry listened, he became quite drowsy. Settling himself in a comfortable position, he put his feet on the hassock, and simply dropped off to sleep. The telephone slipped from his hand.

After a time, the lady on the other end of the line realized she was getting no response from Mr. T. Frantically, she called his name, but August Terry slept on. Finally, she hung up the phone, tried to dial another number but found her own line still connected. Clearly, something had happened to Mr. T.

Hurriedly, she ran to a neighbor's house and called the police.

The big moment, we learned, was at the hospital when the doctor rushed in to examine poor Mr. Terry. After checking the patient's vital signs and learning from the ambulance attendant how Mr. Terry had been found comfortably seated in his favorite chair, the phone dangling in mid-air, the doctor, with an amused look on his face, assured all concerned that Mr. T. was in no danger at all. He was, in fact, merely enjoying the blessings of a very good sleeping pill.

Thereupon, the ambulance attendants loaded up Mr. Terry for one more ride—no sirens this time—and quietly drove him home where he continued his night in peace.

Needless to say that after that memorable night, Mr. T. was fairly famous around town, receiving much attention, which he found pleasurable.

Everything has changed.

JPs were voted out and Mr. Terry has advanced to a "higher court." The old house on the corner has been sold. It's a canary yellow now, and there's a concrete walk in place of the flagstone steps that once led up to the wide front porch. But oh! how good to remember the excitement on our street in the days when August Terry held court.

BONNIE ROSE

Anne H. Norris

BONNIE ROSE was a very sad little girl. She never wore a happy face.

She lived in a pretty red brick house. She had a wonderful mother and father and four big brothers who loved her very much. She had a dog named Barney and a cat named Patches. She had her own room and lots of dolls and a shelf filled with all kinds of books. But Bonnie Rose was not a happy little girl.

She went to a brand new school, only a few blocks from her house. It was a beautiful school, with pink walls and bright colors in all the classrooms. Miss Smith was a wonderful teacher, and Bonnie Rose liked the girls in her room. But she didn't like the boys very much. That was part of the reason she was not happy. The boys teased her.

Bonnie Rose was sure everything would be better if only she had a different name. She didn't know another girl with a name like Bonnie Rose. The four other girls who sat at her table were named Allison and Jennifer and Joanna and Amanda. They had nice names, and they had nicknames too. Sometimes Allison was called Al, and Jennifer was Jen. Lots of people called Joanna "Jo Jo" and most everyone called Amanda "Mandy." She didn't have a nickname, although sometimes her daddy called her "Rosie" and would sing a little song he made up about "Sweet Rosie is My Pretty Posey." She thought Rosie was even worse than Bonnie Rose.

It really was all her mother's fault because she was the one who had named her. Her father said he always gave that job to her mother because he wasn't good at names. Her mother hadn't done too bad with names for her brothers. She couldn't understand why she hadn't picked out a better name for her.

Her oldest brother was named Robert, although most of his friends called him Bob or Bobby. At home he usually was called Bubba. That was because when Norris, who was her next–to–the–oldest brother, was learning to talk, he couldn't say "brother" and it sounded like "Bubba."

After Robert and Norris, the next baby was named Adam. Bonnie Rose really liked that name even if she never called him Adam. He was big and strong and liked to play football. His friends said he could run down the football field very fast, charging ahead like a buffalo. So they gave him the name "Buffalo." It soon was shortened to just Buff, which is what Bonnie Rose always called him.

Her youngest brother was named Frank, but everyone called him Nip. He got that nickname from his brothers because his black curly hair was always tangled. When their mother combed his hair, he would cry and say she was pulling his nips. The other boys thought this was funny and began calling him Nip.

With four boys already, her mother was sure the fifth baby would be another boy. She had the name picked out. She was going to name this one John.

What a surprise! She had a baby girl. But she didn't have any names picked out for a girl. Maybe she would name her for Grandmother Dora. But Grandmother Dora didn't like that idea. She said when she was a little girl, the boys at school would tease her and call her Dumb Dora and she wasn't dumb at all. Grandmother Dora said to please not give her that name.

Maybe she would name her for Aunt Mary. Mother thought that would make Aunt Mary very happy.

"Oh, no," said Aunt Mary, "please don't name your pretty baby for me." Aunt Mary said when she was a little girl, the boys at school liked to tease her and say, "Mary, Mary, quite contrary, how does your garden grow?" Just like in the nursery rhyme. "Besides," said Aunt Mary, "there are a lot of girls named Mary. Give your baby a name that is different."

Of course Bonnie Rose knew how she finally got her name. She had been told about that since she was just a baby. Her daddy was so happy to have a little girl, and he loved her mother so much. He bought her mother a dozen beautiful pink roses. Mama said she had looked at her baby's tiny little mouth, pink and sort of puckered up like a little pink rose bud, and she said, "I will name her Rose." Because Mama thought she was so pretty, she chose the name Bonnie, which means beautiful. Bonnie Rose.

Bonnie Rose didn't like her name and she certainly didn't think of herself as beautiful. She wished she looked more like her brothers. They all had brown eyes and dark hair, just like Daddy. In the summer when they were outside a lot, they all got wonderful suntans.

She was just like her mother. She had blue eyes and blond hair and had to put on lots of suntan lotion when she went to the beach and always wear a big hat to keep the sun from shining on her face. She never got a suntan. She got freckles.

She hated her freckles even more than she hated her name. At recess, the boys would call out, "Bonnie Rose, Bonnie Rose, you've got freckles on your nose!" And she would cry.

Her mother tried to tell her that her freckles made her pretty, but she still hated them. She did feel bad, though, when her mother reminded her that she had freckles too. Bonnie Rose certainly didn't think her mother was ugly. She was just about the most beautiful mother anyone ever had. And she guessed it made her mother sort of sad when she said she hated her name because it was her mother who had named her.

Then one day right after the Christmas holidays a new family moved into the white house at the end of Bonnie Rose's street. There was a girl who was just Bonnie Rose's age and was in her room at school. The girl's name was Lily!

Bonnie Rose wondered if Lily's mother had thought her baby looked like a Lily when she was born. It almost made her giggle, but she didn't say anything because she didn't want to hurt Lily's feelings.

She was sure she knew why her name wasn't Bonnie Lily. She probably wasn't pretty when she was born because Bonnie Rose didn't think Lily was pretty now. In fact, Bonnie Rose thought, she looks a lot like me. Her hair is blonde, and her eyes are blue. We are almost the same size, but Lily has lots more freckles. There was another big difference, too. Lily always wore a happy face.

At first some of the boys teased Lily and called her Freckle Face, but Lily never cried. In fact, she laughed right with them. She said she had moved there from the country, where her father had a dairy farm. She said one of his cows had spit bran in her face! That made all the boys and girls laugh. Soon no one teased her at all and everyone wanted to be her "best friend."

When they were walking to school one morning, Bonnie Rose asked Lily how she could always be so happy, especially with so many freckles. And didn't she just hate having the same name as a flower?

Lily said she used to wish her name was Sandra or Kathy like one of her cousins, but she really didn't mind being Lily. She had been born on Easter Sunday, and her mother had been given a pot of beautiful Easter lilies. They had filled the room with their sweet perfume and were so lovely, and of course, that is how she got her name.

"Just think," said Lily, "suppose I had been born on Christmas. Someone might have brought my mother a pot of poinsettias, the beautiful red Christmas flowers. Think what my mother might have named me then! I would much rather be named Lily than Poinsettia." This made both girls laugh.

Lily told Bonnie Rose that for a long time she didn't like her freckles. She had scrubbed them with kitchen cleanser and once even tried fingernail polish remover, which had made blisters on her face. She had washed her face with lemon juice because someone had told her that would bleach out her freckles, but that didn't work either.

Then her favorite uncle had come to visit them, and he had told her how much he liked her freckles and how he had wanted freckles when he was a little boy. He had said that freckles are just kisses from angels. Of course, she knew that wasn't really true, but she liked to pretend it was.

Her uncle told her that it really doesn't matter how one looks on the outside. The important thing is how one is on the inside and how one acts.

Bonnie Rose thought about that a lot after she had gone to bed that night. She really had not understood what her grandmother meant when she often would say, "Pretty is as pretty does." Now she knew. It means that you are pretty if you act pretty. No matter how pretty you look, if you don't act nice, you won't have friends and no one will like you. That must be right because Lily wasn't a very pretty girl, just to look at her, but once you got to know her, you really, really liked her. You didn't even think about how she looked. You just saw her big smile and heard her happy laugh. And you loved her a lot when she gave you a big hug or held your hand as you walked to school.

Bonnie Rose went to sleep with a happy feeling and a smile on her face because she had decided that she would try to be like her best friend Lily.

The next day Miss Smith asked all the boys and girls to take turns standing in front of the class and telling what makes them happy.

Joe was happy because his father was going to take him fishing on Saturday. Billy was going camping. Joyce had a new dress that had pink flowers on the skirt, and she was going to wear it to her cousin's wedding. Paul was happy because his mother had bought him a new fish for his aquarium.

Soon it was time for those at Bonnie Rose's table. Allison said she was happy because she was going to have a birthday party the next week. Jennifer was happy because she was going on an airplane, all by herself, to visit her grandparents in Florida. Joanna's cat had five new kittens and that made her happy. Amanda's mother was going to take her to the zoo on Saturday.

Then Miss Smith said, "Bonnie Rose, tell us what makes you happy."

Bonnie Rose almost danced as she hurried to the front of the room. She looked at Lily and with a big smile, she said:

> "I'm happy because my name is Bonnie Rose,
> And I have freckles on my nose."

MUSIC AND THE SCENT OF LILACS

Ruth Crenshaw

COULD you believe it possible that the bond of love, music and the scent of lilacs could be so strong that it would transcend time, distance, and even death? That two hearts could be so tied together that there would be no separation? There is one who believes it truly. Here is her story.

Music came into her life early. You might say she was born to it. They said, "When that one was born, she came with a song instead of a cry." Not true, of course. Still, her first memories are of singing. If she didn't know the words, she made up sounds to fit the rhythm of the melodies. Tunes came easily, and later, as she learned words, the tunes became songs. She sang any song: old ones, songs of the day, and especially hymns, for her family kept church schedules, rain or shine.

They were a musical family. Her mother played the little church organ, her father lent his rich bass to the choir, and both sisters played piano and sang. Her brother, although shy about it, joined in when the family had their late evening songfests on the side screened porch.

By the age or two and a half or three, someone stood her on the piano at church, and she sang her first solo. It was a heady sensation, a feeling she didn't understand, but she liked it. It was a source of amusement for her family when, with a serious expression, she would burst out with "Tiptoe Through the Tulips," or the sad ballad of "Barbara Allen."

Those were the depression years, and after the grandmother's death, the family left the small Mississippi town for better times to live in Tennessee. It was then the real joy of music came into a life, through a teacher whom everyone called "Miss Mary."

Miss Mary was the pianist at their church and taught piano and voice. She had heard the child sing in church and her first solo at school, where she sang Topsy's Song from *Uncle Tom's Cabin*. In a talk with her mother, Miss Mary pressed her to begin piano lessons for the child. And so began the relationship between a teacher and a little girl.

One Saturday morning when she was eleven—she remembers it well—Miss Mary had asked her to come by for a chat. When she arrived they went into the music room with its chintz–covered sofa and organdy curtains fluttering at broad windows. Shelves of music lined the wall from floor to ceiling. Miss Mary sat down at the piano and began running scales. The picture is still vivid to the child—Miss Mary with her silver hair (they said she grayed prematurely) with setting combs in place and the luxurious bun at the back; Miss Mary with her deep blue eyes and a smile like the sun breaking through. But it was her beautiful, strong hands on the keyboard and her velvet contralto voice that held the young girl spellbound.

"I thought it time we started a little singing," she heard her teacher say.

The piano lessons had been pleasant enough, but the young girl was impatient to begin her voice training. She had become convinced she would never become a pianist, especially since her fingers were too small to reach an octave on the keyboard.

Now she and her teacher settled into a routine, one lesson of piano and one of voice each week, winter and summer. For these lessons, her feet fairly flew to get to Miss Mary's house—always early. The door would be opened by the housekeeper, Elzora—Elzora with her stiff braids all askew, her mulatto face with its open grin, apron loosely tied, standing in shiny black rubber overshoes she wore the year round. In winter she just added men's socks. She greeted each student with affection, for she was part of their musical experience.

Regularly, after a summer's lesson, Elzora presided over the serving of ice cream in the back garden. It was here the lilacs grew—banks and banks, bending, almost dipping into the small fish pond near the fence. Tall baskets of these delicate lavender blossoms filled the stage in the school auditorium for the annual recital, a showcase for the students' progress, or lack of it.

Recitals were events of both anticipation and dread. For the young girl, it was the fear of the proverbial piano solos. The moment she sat down to play, her hands became disconnected from the rest of her body and refused to respond to signals from her brain. Often she wished she could leave the stage and let her hands finish by themselves. Her joy from these recitals came when she walked on the stage to sing. It gave her a pleasure she would cherish for the rest of her life.

Lesson by lesson, her world of music expanded as her voice developed. She sang her way from Romberg to Verdi, from Gershwin and Porter to Kahn and Berlin. With the introduction of each composer to the young girl, Miss Mary added the background of how, when, and why the song had been written. One story Miss Mary told was the anecdote involving Otto Harbach and Oscar Hammerstein, who were writing the lyrics for Rudolph Friml's *Rosemarie*. They were stuck on a duet suitable for Jeanette MacDonald and Nelson Eddy. The two composers were both quite weary, and they had imbibed a little too much. Taking refuge in Central Park, one lying on a park bench called to the other, "Yoo hoo! I'm calling you."

The other would answer back as an echo from across the park. That's how *Indian Love Call* came to be written.

The young girl had been growing up, now an adolescent facing a different world. Both her parents had died, the country was deep in a war, and there were decisions to be made about her future. More and more she turned to those sessions by the piano. Miss Mary had not only taught her how to deliver a song before an audience, she had also taught her to use songs to sustain her through those difficult days. She found a song to meet each situation—for the blues, for painful memories, for hope and for dreaming.

When her father died, she had made the decision to seek a career in nursing. With the war raging, the needs were great. The day after graduation, she had her last singing lesson and told Miss Mary she would be leaving soon.

"Of course," her teacher said, "that isn't what I had wanted for you. But I know you will do well. Just remember—whatever happens, sing a song."

Through the years they kept in touch, and the little girl, now grown, kept singing. She married, and there were responsibilities: lullabies to sing, the choir and the chorus. With the ups and downs, there was always a song to sing. There also were lilacs in her garden, but the soil seemed unable to nourish them, and they refused to grow. If they died, she kept replanting.

It was late spring several years ago when a friend from back home called to tell her Miss Mary had a brain tumor and was in a local hospital. She rushed to see her former teacher. Miss Mary had just returned to her room after a treatment. One side of her lovely silver hair had been shaved away, and the skin was marked with crimson where the X–ray had focused. She was far too ill for anything except a hand clasp and a smile. Not time for anything except "I love you." Miss Mary's daughter–in–law, Ellen, whispered she would be taking her home with her that afternoon.

Two weeks passed. One morning while sitting at her desk, she suddenly thought, "I must send flowers to Miss Mary." She looked at the clock. It was ten o'clock. The flower shops would be open.

She wanted lilacs, but they were not to be had, and in the end she settled for roses.

Early the next morning, the telephone rang. It was Ellen. "I'm sorry to tell you; Miss Mary died at ten o'clock yesterday morning. Thank you for the lovely flowers. She would have loved them."

With tears streaming down her cheeks, she went out to the garden. And there on her puny lilac bush, which had never bloomed, hung one perfect blossom. The bush never bloomed again.

Call it coincidence, call it whatever you will. Yet each spring when lilacs bloom, the songs return, and Miss Mary is there.

THE TREASURE CHEST

Anne H. Norris

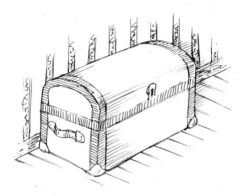

SCHOOL was still out for the Christmas holidays. When I answered the knock at my front door, there stood my little neighbor, Jennifer, and her two visiting cousins from Ohio, Joanna and Amanda. Earlier I had watched them playing in the cove and had remarked to my husband that little Jennifer, a dimpled blue-eyed blonde, was such a contrast to her cousins, who had shiny black hair and big brown eyes.

My husband and I have no children of our own, but we became Aunt Rubye and Uncle Charlie to Jennifer soon after her family moved into the house next door.

Jennifer, who had just turned seven and was in the second grade, had taught me a lot of things, like how to play Old Maid and Go Fishing. And I had never had trouble finding a helper when baking cookies or making popcorn balls.

"Please, Aunt Rubye," she said when I opened the door, "will you open your treasure chest and let my cousins see Sarah Jane?"

First, I should explain that I really don't have a treasure chest. It's just a small, very old trunk in which I keep "Sarah Jane" and some other things that have little or no real value, but hold too many memories for me to throw them away.

I invited my young guests in and we went to the back bedroom to open the "treasure chest."

Jennifer reached down and lovingly patted Sarah Jane and, with great importance, explained to Amanda and Joanna that Aunte Rubye had had this doll for a long, long time—since she was seven years old herself. Jennifer's cousins seemed mightily impressed, looking from the doll to me, as if to say, "Can the doll really be THAT old?"

"Is she more than fifty years old?", asked Joanna.

"Oh, yes," I said with a smile. They listened attentively as I told them how I came to get Sarah Jane.

My family were sharecroppers, and we lived in a rural area of Arkansas. I explained to my little friends about sharecroppers, who are just what the name implies. They live on someone else's farm and "share the crop." I was a child during the Great Depression of the 1930s, and my family's share was a place to live and, most of the time, enough food for our table. When crops are not good, sharecroppers often move. We moved a lot. I was happy if I got to stay in one school the entire year.

I started the second grade at Oak Hill School, which was just a one–room school. There were about thirty children, ranging from the first through the eighth grades, all taught by Mr. Miller. Only later did I realize what a wonderful, dedicated teacher he was, coming to school early to make a fire in that old potbellied stove during winter months when few, if any, of us had clothes warm enough or shoes without holes in the soles.

I don't recall that discipline was ever a problem because most of us were eager to learn. It was exciting to hear about faraway countries and read those wonderful books in Mr. Miller's cabinet. Sometimes he would let us take a book home to share with our parents.

And what fun I had at recess! At home there was no one for me to play with except for my three-year-old sister, but at school there were other children. Best of all, there was Jesse. Jesse Cline was my idol. His hair was cropped short all around, but it fell on his forehead in a mass of blond curls.

No one ever had a crush like I had on Jesse. I was sure we would grow up and marry and live happily ever after. Actually, I don't think Jesse was aware of my affection. I was new in that school and very shy. I didn't yet have any close friends, so I kept my secret love for Jesse all to myself. One day, though, I did hit him with a snowball. I thought that should let him know that I really liked him a lot.

Christmas was approaching, and Mr. Miller had us all draw names. I was so excited when I found out that Jesse had drawn my name. I knew without a shadow of a doubt that I would get something real nice from Jesse. My daddy and mother had already explained to me that all those wonderful toys in the Sears, Roebuck catalog had been promised to other children and that Santa Claus would never be able to get all the way out to our house.

I had looked under the bed, though, and found a corn shuck doll that my mother had made for me and what looked like a doll bed that I thought my daddy had made. We would go to the church on Christmas Eve, and all us children would get an apple and an orange, some raisins, and maybe a candy cane. What I wanted more than anything, though, was a real doll—a real store–bought doll. "Someday, Rubye, someday. You just wait. Someday you will have your doll," my mother said. I knew "someday" wasn't going to be anytime soon.

It really didn't matter so much that I wouldn't be getting a real doll for Christmas because Jesse had drawn my name. I knew I wouldn't get a doll from him, but maybe a box of crayons. Could it be that he might even give me some cutout paper dolls like I had seen in Mr. Murphy's store? Every night I dreamed about what my present might be.

The big boys at school had cut down a cedar tree and made a stand for it. With the skimpy side turned to the wall, it looked just wonderful in the corner farthest from the stove. We had decorated it with strings of popcorn and red berries and paper chains. One of the big girls had even made a bright star for the very top of the tree. I thought it must be the most beautiful Christmas tree in the whole wide world.

Mr. Miller had said we could bring our present for the person whose name we had drawn any day during the week before the Christmas holidays. By the middle of the week, there were a lot of presents under the tree. I watched every morning to see what Jesse would bring, but he seemed to always come in empty-handed. I was sure he had slipped something in when I wasn't looking so he could surprise me. I could hardly wait until the gifts would be given out.

Finally the day came. Mr. Miller read Christmas stories to us and we played some games and sang carols. I was so excited. Even my biscuit and fried egg lunch tasted better than usual.

At last it was time! Mr. Miller read the name on each present, and the children went up, one by one, to get their gifts. That is, everyone went but me.

Mr. Miller surely did not realize he had not called my name—that there was no present under the tree for me.

School was dismissed and the other children ran out with shouts of "Merry Christmas" and "Happy New Year." I hurried out too, but I didn't run with the others. I hid behind the schoolhouse until everyone had gone. I didn't want anyone to see me crying. My heart was broken. I could not believe Jesse had not brought a present for me. He had run out of the schoolhouse, right by me, without a word. How could he be so mean?

My mother didn't know what was wrong, but one look at my tear–stained face and red eyes and she just threw open her arms. Between sobs, I told her what had happened. Nothing could be worse than being the only one in school without a present under the tree, especially knowing it was Jesse who had drawn my name. He hadn't brought me anything at all, and I had loved him so much, even if no one but me knew it.

Mama didn't have an answer, only loving arms that held me close until my tears stopped.

I wasn't hungry at supper that night. Daddy tried to cheer me. He talked about the Christmas program at church and what fun we would have together with our neighbors, but it didn't seem important to me anymore.

Mama was baking cookies when I got up the next morning. Usually I was right there to help roll out the dough, but even that didn't hold any interest for me.

All I could think about was Jesse, who had betrayed me.

We were just finishing supper that night when there was a knock at our door. We didn't have many visitors, especially at night. Daddy went to the door and then he called me.

There stood Mr. Cline, Jesse's father, with a sack in his hand. As he handed it to me, he leaned down and hugged me real tight. "Rubye," he said, "this is from Jesse. He wanted to put it under the tree at school, but there just was no money to buy anything for you until I got paid today. I'm sorry your present is late."

Mr. Cline came in to get warm before he walked the eight miles back to his house. He watched with Mama and Daddy as I opened the sack. There was my first real, store-bought doll, with golden hair and eyes that opened and closed. My dream come true! My Sarah Jane. Never had I been so happy.

When Jesse's father had gone, I heard Daddy and Mama talking about Mr. Cline's coming in the cold to bring me such an expensive gift. The Clines were sharecroppers too. Besides Jesse, there were several other children in the family. None of them was likely to get anything for Christmas as nice as my doll.

Perhaps Jennifer was right in calling my old trunk a treasure chest for surely the doll it holds is a true treasure. It mended the broken heart of a little girl. More than that, over the years Sarah Jane has been a reminder of the true spirit of Christmas, that of love and sacrifice. The spirit that puts a song in our hearts and causes us to sing with gladness, "Joy to the world, the Lord has come."

THE ALTAR SOCIETY MEETING

Madge H. Lewis

MY HOME in the early 1930s was in Helena, Arkansas, a small town on the Mississippi River not far from Memphis. I liked living there except for a few friends who used to brag, brag, brag about their important relatives. One had an uncle who was a U.S. Senator from Kentucky; another had an older brother who had earned a scholarship to Princeton; the snootiest one had an aunt who had made her debut in New York society and later married the Duke of Bottomly and lived in a castle in England.

I racked my brain to come up with one—just one—relative who had achieved something notable. After careful consideration, at the age of ten, I decided that it was wiser not to discuss my kinfolk and to pretend they didn't exist. Never was I more certain of this than the day my mother hosted the Altar Society meeting.

Mama wanted more than anything to be president of St. Mary's Altar Society. She had served on several committees and had made reports at the meetings. Yet so far, she had not been nominated for the office and was discouraged until one day the outgoing president asked her to be the hostess for the spring meeting. She felt this might be a sign they were considering her.

For two weeks prior to the meeting our house was scrubbed, rubbed and polished to a state of cleanliness it had never known before. Mammy Lou had worked for Mama since before I was born and handled our house and everyone in it like she was Grant at Vicksburg giving orders to his troops. She was short, with rolls of fat cascading from her chin to her chubby ankles. Woe betide any slackers such as my younger brother Budgie and me if we didn't pitch in when tasks were handed out for an important project such as the Altar Society meeting.

Eighteen year old Martin Williams also worked for Mama. He had lived in our basement room as long as I could remember. Daddy, on his way home from the office one wintry day, had found him huddled against a building for warmth.

"Young man, you'd better head for home. A snow storm is brewing and your parents will be worried about you," Daddy told him.

"I ain't got no parents, mistah, or no home either to go to. I'm a orphan."

Daddy told us later he could not resist the big brown eyes that looked up at him so he brought him home to stay with us until the weather cleared. Mama and Mammy Lou placed a cot in the basement where it was cozy and warm All through that harsh winter Martin stoked the furnace and gradually took on other chores until Mama said he'd made a place for himself. He was twelve years old when he came to our house on that snowy day; he'd been with us ever since. Martin was small and wiry, with golden brown skin and a ready smile that displayed his shining white teeth.

Mammy Lou and Martin were both "nigras." We weren't allowed to use the other "n" word and "African–American" hadn't been thought of yet. We could, however, say they were colored, but Mama thought it pleased them more to be called "nigras." No matter what they were called, Mammy Lou and Martin were as much a part of our family as though they had been born into it.

To get ready for the spring Altar Society meeting, Martin and Budgie worked on the flower beds and put big circles of mulch and manure around the dogwood and the flowering crab trees. The jonquils were just beginning to peep through the ground and the forsythia and azalea bushes were loaded with buds.

"Missy," Martin said to Mama, "it's gonna be a sight to see when your ladies come to that meetin' in two weeks. Them plants are gonna make their eyes pop outta their heads—all that red and yeller—and the yard green and clipped like a high–toned barber done took his shears to it."

Mammy Lou took down the organdy curtains throughout the house and washed them, calling out to Budgie and me to see the gray, almost black, color of the soapy water as she swished them around in the big washtub in the back yard.

"Lawsey, your mama ain't havin' me do this one day too early. These curtains was jes waitin' for a good washin'."

After she rinsed them two or three times, she transferred them to a black iron pot filled with starchy water. I helped her wring out the curtains and put them on the wooden stretchers with little pins all around them. I had such a good time helping Mammy Lou that day.

"Ain't nobody at that meetin' gonna say that your mama's curtains ain't clean. Um-m! Jes smell that starch. Ain't nuthin' in this world smells as good as clean organdy curtains!"

The next day Mammy Lou and Martin washed the windows with Bon Ami, she on the inside and he on the outside. Mammy Lou being bossy like she was, gave Martin a piece of her mind when he missed a spot.

"Martin Williams," she shook her finger at him, "you done missed this whole pane. Watch what ye'r doin', boy. We gotta make these here windows sparkle!"

While the housecleaning was going on, Mama was baking the refreshments that would be served on the important day. The ladies of Helena ate dinner at noon with their husbands, so everything to be served was in the dessert category.

First, Mama made date sticks because they would last the longest. Then she made divinity, orange pecans, macaroons, oatmeal cookies, petits–fours, charlotte russe and Boston Cream Pie. Every room in the house was filled with the aroma of delectable goodies.

The moment arrived. We, like the house, had been scrubbed, starched and whisked into shape. I waited at the door beside Mama to greet her guests, and Budgie was sent outside to spend the rest of the afternoon with Martin.

The ladies of St. Mary's Altar Society arrived grandly, one after the other, bedecked in their best finery with matching hats and gloves. They didn't look as nice as Mama, though; she wore her dark hair in a full chignon at her nape, and small tendrils escaped around her face, giving her such a young and pretty look. She had on her shiny rose-colored silk dress and her brown eyes shone with the pleasure of welcoming her guests. I had the duty of escorting the ladies to the master bedroom where they placed their purses on the bed before joining the others in the living room for the meeting.

One of the guests, Mrs. Henderson, had been asked to preside at the silver tea service and she handled it with grace, with her broad-brimmed hat still skewered securely to the hair atop her head. Mama had asked me to help with the serving, and I placed a date stick on each plate with a special sterling silver cookie server. I felt important until I had been bumped by several oversized rear ends as they rounded the corner of the table.

When the ladies had consumed everything on their fully laden plates, Mammy Lou and I removed the dishes and the meeting started. It had barely begun when we heard laughter and footsteps on the front porch.

"Surprise! Surprise!" shouted my 24–year–old cousin Ellen as she barged into the meeting room, a baby on one hip, a bag filled with diapers and bottles hanging over her shoulder and resting on the other. Following on her heels were her two–year–old identical twins—so alike that no one, not even the parents, could tell them apart. Consequently, they were called This One and That One.

Then, Lord help us, Ellen's mother, Aunt Clara, came through the door, expressing surprise in her loud voice that Mama had company. She was married to Mama's brother, Uncle John.

Mama was making a valiant effort to be warm and hospitable to her unexpected company. After all, they were her relatives and she realized that they had driven from Marianna, Arkansas, over a dusty gravel road to get here. But the shocked look on her face almost gave her away when she spied her sister Dora bringing up the rear.

Aunt Dora. The last person in the world Mama wanted to introduce to the ladies of St. Mary's Altar Society. We called her Dodie, at her request, because it made her sound younger than she really was. The shame of the whole matter was that Dodie was d-i-v-o-r-c-e-d. And she worked in an office where she was the only woman. And she lived in Little Rock—a big city filled with all kinds of temptations.

Mama closed her eyes for a moment, and I thought she must be trying to think of the right words. I knew, in her heart, she wanted to say, "Go someplace else for an hour or two." But Mama was a true lady so she kept her thoughts to herself.

I took the relatives into the bedroom so they could place their possessions on the bed. Cousin Ellen laid the baby down in the middle of the purses and changed his diaper. Then they all trooped to our spanking clean bathroom where the new lace-edged cloths and towels had been laid out. They said they were going to wash the Arkansas dust off their hands and faces..

"Lawsey me," Mammy Lou moaned as she heard them going down the hall.. "Missy been working two whole weeks to make this here affair jes perfeck. She gonna have a heart attack."

When our relatives felt that they were presentable, they went back to the living room and sat in on the meeting as though they were members of the Altar Society. This One and That One played in the middle of the floor with some blocks I had found for them, and Ellen's smallest—thank you, Jesus—slept soundly on her shoulder.

Aunt Clara, who was sitting next to me, seemed fidgety and left the meeting two or three times to go into the bedroom. In the middle of an important motion being made by one of the Altar Society ladies, a terrible thought struck me. What was Aunt Clara doing, going back and forth to the bedroom so many times? My face began to flush as the truth dawned! Mama had explained to us one day, after the mysterious disappearance of an emerald ring, that poor Aunt Clara had a sickness called "kleptomania," and we must be careful about leaving valuables around when she was here. After that, we had secretly called her Clara the Klep.

Had Mama left something out in the bedroom? But Mammy Lou had put nearly everything away in her straightening up before the meeting. So what could Aunt Clara be doing in the bedroom—the bedroom with all those purses!

I tiptoed out of the meeting and peeked through the bedroom door. There was Aunt Clara opening one purse after another and stuffing a five dollar bill from each one into the pocket of her dress.

She looked up and her beady eyes met mine just after she closed the last purse. The expression on her face said, "Don't you dare squeal on me, you little brat."

I guess she knew I loved Mama too much to add embarrassment to the gathering in which she obviously had so much pride. Aunt Clara and I went back to our chairs without saying a word and I sat right next to her trying to keep my anger under control. There goes Mama's chance to be president, I thought, and knew how humiliated she would be when the ladies put their heads together and realized money had been stolen at our house. They might even suspect me!

The meeting came to an end with a prayer; heads were bowed and eyes closed. As we prayed together I glanced once more at Aunt Clara, leaning closer to her and silently formed a prayer of my own. Afterwards the ladies of the Altar Society pronounced the meeting a great success—especially the delicious food. I volunteered to get their purses for them, my heart pounding wildly. I could hear their farewells when I was in the bedroom. They were gracious in telling Mama's relatives how happy they were to have met them.

Dodie was sophisticated from having lived in Little Rock, and she returned the compliments nicely. I pictured Ellen's being too busy with the baby and This One and That One to say anything because I didn't hear a word out of her.

But Aunt Clara went on and on in her loud voice saying she had never had a more enjoyable afternoon and invited everyone to visit her in Marianna. As I returned to the living room to hand out the purses she was saying, "I found so much in common with you nice ladies. Don't forget my invitation, now. I'll be lookin' for you."

After the last Altar Society lady left Mama said, "Can you believe it?" as she threw her arms around me. "Mrs. Henderson whispered to me that I will be nominated for the presidency at the next meeting. It doesn't seem possible that it has finally happened!"

"I'm happy, Mama. You'll make a great president," I said aloud but I sent these words upward: "Thank you, Jesus, for helping me get that money out of Clara the Klep's pocket and back into all those purses. I had to work fast—but we pulled it off, didn't we?"

A GARDEN FOR MAMA

Malra Treece

BEN SAT on the front steps of the gray shotgun house on a narrow lot. The front yard consisted only of packed black dirt.

Mama had told him that some people out in the country, where she grew up, always swept their yards clean, leaving not a sprig of anything green. They thought that was how neat front yards ought to look. The people who used to live in this house must have had the same crazy idea.

Mama said she likes growing things, green grass and pretty flowers and maybe a tomato plant or two, and green peppers to eat with black–eyed peas. She meant to have all these things, sometime, even though the house was not theirs, just rented.

They had been glad to move into the house. It wasn't much—Ben knew that—but it was better than the little old apartment in the housing project where they lived before. Ben hadn't known what was meant by a "shotgun house." Mama said that was just a slang name for a long, narrow house with all the rooms lined up, front to back, so that a shell from a shotgun could go through the front door and out the back door. It seemed pretty silly to Ben, but there were still a lot of things that he did not understand a bit.

A month after they moved in, Mama got sick and had to quit work as a night cook at Shoney's, and then she got worse and had to go to the hospital. But she was going to be all right. She told him so before she left.

Uncle Wash, as all the other neighbors called him, lived in another shotgun house next door. Ben and his mother called him Mr. Washington, at least to his face, in order to sound respectful. Uncle Wash owned his house, free and clear, and didn't have to pay any rent. Ben couldn't imagine how anybody could ever have enough money to pay for a whole house. Uncle Wash told him that he bought the house a long time ago and paid for it by the month, just like paying rent, when he was working as a janitor at the church.

Uncle Wash's yard didn't look like much, either, but he had a patch of tall purple flowers—his mother said they were irises—beside his front step. Needles from a bent–over pine tree covered some of the black bare dirt, and there was a pile of rocks that Uncle Wash called his rock garden, although it was just a pile of rocks without a smidgen of anything else.

Uncle Wash came from his house next door. "You hungry, Ben?"

"Yes sir, a little." He was nearly always hungry, but he was beginning to get used to it.

"I brought you a big plate full of catfish—caught them myself—and a pile of cornbread, and a cup of coffee. You drink coffee yet?"

"No sir, but it's time to start. Thank you, Mr. Washington."

"Just call me Uncle Wash. Everybody else does."

"Yes sir, but Mama says it's not really respectful, and that you're a good old man."

"Well, even a good old man can be called Uncle Wash."

"This is the very best breakfast I ever had in my whole life," Ben said. "Thank you, Uncle Wash."

"You're welcome. When you get full, I'll be walking you to school."

"You don't need to walk me to school. I'm in the fifth grade. Mama just walks with me so that we can talk. I can walk by myself."

"I be walking you to school."

"You don't need to."

"Maybe I want to talk to you, too. I get lonesome living all by my own self."

"Well, OK. Let me get my books."

"Brush your teeth and put on a sweater. The wind is blowing up cold."

"Yes sir."

They walked for a few minutes without speaking. "What do you and your mama talk about when you walk to school?"

"About all the big houses we pass, starting two blocks from here. They are made of brick and have all kinds of flowers around them, especially now in the spring. Big flowers, little flowers, purple, white, pink, red, trees full of flowers, blue flowers..."

"What else to you all talk about?"

"We talk about my lessons. I teach her things and she teaches me things. She didn't get to go to school much, but she's smart."

"Yeah, I know. Your mama is smart. You got that right. Pretty, too."

"She can read all the hard words in my books, and she can do long division in a flash."

"Yeah. I can figure pretty good, too."

"My mama must know the name of every kind of flower in the world. She has taught me the names of all the flowers in the he yards that we pass. First it was the crocuses, all colors, and purple hyacinths, and millions of yellow daffodils, before they stopped blooming and fell over."

"What are them purple things there?"

"They are irises, Uncle Wash. You have some in your yard."

"Is that what they are? They've been there all the time. Somebody else planted them or they just come up."

"Some people call them flags. They stand tall like a flagpole and wave their blooms in the air."

"I know them bushes," Uncle Wash said. "They're azaleas. I used to have a white one in my yard, but it died."

"Yes sir. And look at the tulips and the pansies. The tulips must be a late variety."

"Yeah, Ben."

"Look, Uncle Wash, at the dandelions there behind the iron fence. Nothing but dandelions all over the place. Don't they look pretty, all spread out all over, like a bunch of stars fell down and filled up the yard."

"Them is weeds, Ben. Most people pull them up."

"Pull them up? Pull them up? Why?"

"They say they choke out the grass."

"They pull them up and throw them away?"

"Yeah. Or they mow them down."

"I don't see any difference between a pretty flower and a pretty weed. Anyway, what is a weed?"

"Ask your mama. Look, Ben, across from the school house. That white woman is pulling up something now. Probably dandelions."

Ben ran to the woman's yard, being careful to stop on the sidewalk. "Ma'am, what are you doing?"

She stopped to look him over. "Can't you see? I'm pulling up dandelions."

"Why?"

"Why? So my yard will look nice. But it's too much trouble. I guess I'll just mow them down and let them come back up again."

"Are you just going to throw them away?" Ben asked.

"Why—yes, of course." She was looking at him funny.

"Could I have the dandelions, please?" Ben asked.

"You want the dandelions?"

"Yes'm, seeing that you are going to throw them out anyway. I'll pull them after school, or dig them out if you want, free of charge. Is that all right?"

"Why on earth would you ever want that?"

"So that I can make a flower garden for my mama. She is sick in the hospital, but maybe she will come home pretty soon. I want it to be a surprise. I will keep her garden a secret until the very day she comes home."

"Does your mother particularly like dandelions?"

"I never asked her, but she likes all kinds of flowers. She ain't—hasn't had any for a long time."

"Well..."

"I'll help him," Uncle Wash said. "We will keep everything nice and neat."

"It's an awful job," the woman said. "I'm tired already. Look at this big yard. You don't know what you're getting into."

"That's all right, Ma'am," Uncle Wash said. "We will dig every one of them things out by the roots and tote them off in my wheelbarrow."

"Well," the woman said. "I guess it's all right."

"I'll meet you here right after school," Uncle Wash said to Ben.

At three o'clock Uncle Wash was waiting. He had brought his wheelbarrow, Ben's old red wagon, and two new trowels from the hardware store. "Them are trowels," he explained to Ben. "Little shovels. You know how to use them?"

"No, but I learn fast."

"I bought us candy bars, too, and sandwiches and apples."

They worked until the daylight was about gone. As they were leaving, the woman came outside and gave each of them a five dollar bill.

"No, no, ma'am, we don't want money," Ben said. "Just the flowers."

"Take it. You saved me more than a day's work. If you will come back tomorrow and do the back yard, I'll pay you again."

"Yes'm. Thank you, ma'am."

"I'll bet I can find some neighbors around here who will pay you even more," the woman said. "Would you like to do that?"

"Oh, yes. A thousand times yes."

The woman laughed. She looked younger than before. "I also have some white daisies and black-eyed Susans that need dividing, and mums, and I don't know what all. You can put them in your mother's garden if you will dig them up."

"I'll dig them up."

"We'll be rich," Ben said several times on the way home. "I will work every day after school, five time five equals twenty-five dollars a week, and all day on Saturdays. How many weeks do dandelions keep on growing, Uncle Wash?"

"Forever and ever," Uncle Wash replied. "They don't have to be fed or watered or anything else, except left alone. That's why folks call them weeds."

On the morning that Mama came home from the hospital, the black ground of her front yard was covered with the green leaves and yellow flowers of hundreds of dandelions. Globes of gossamer lace sparkled with dew in the early sunlight. Some of the irises from Uncle Wash's yard stood in a bed near the house, along with bunches of daisies and mums, not yet in bloom. Another bed contained two tomato plants and three pepper plants. Beside the front steps was a large azalea, fresh from the nursery, covered with magnificent white blossoms.

Mama stepped slowly from the pickup driven by Uncle Wash's nephew. Her face was gray and she was so thin that her only skirt was way too big. Ben ran to hug her. She held him tight for a long time, gazing into his eyes. Ben gently pulled away. Finally she raised her head.

"Look, Mama. Do you like your yard?"

She didn't answer. She turned her head in order to see each corner of the yard and the azalea, the irises, the daisies, the mums, the peppers, the tomatoes, the many dandelions. She looked happier than Ben had ever seen her before although her eyes sparkled with tears. "How?" she began. "Ben..."

"We dug them up and planted them. Uncle Wash helped. And we even got money!" He pressed a roll of dollar bills into her hand, then stooped to pick a yellow dandelion and one with a perfect globe of silver seeds, ready for blowing.

"Make a wish, Mama, and if you blow them all off, your wish will come true."

Mama blew. Every seed sailed into the morning breeze, into the yard and into Uncle Wash's yard. "Now we will have even more dandelions," she said. "My wish is that I can always live here with you."

Ben and Uncle Wash helped her up the steps and into the old gray house. "It's so wonderful to be home," she said.

AN IMPROBABLE WITCH

Ethel Joyner

MINERVA had never really wanted to be a witch, but that was her heritage. She came from a long line of hideous witches. She hated wearing the pointed black hats and long capes characteristic of wicked witches, and she was revolted by their stringy hair, toothless smiles, wrinkled faces, and cackling laughs. Her coven was noted to be the ugliest and scariest in all witchdom.

Minerva often pondered why the fates had destined her to a life with evil old crones who rode broomsticks on Halloween night to scare the wits out of little children. Her leader, Carlotta, was dismayed that Minerva showed no inclination to be despised and hideous. In fact, she would appear at pre-Halloween parties looking like Alice in Wonderland—petite and pretty. She was not at all like her sisters who were confounded as to how this improbable little witch came to be in their midst.

Minerva's initiation would officially bring her into the coven, and the witches felt great concern that they would become a laughing stock among all of witchdom once it became known that a beautiful creature, claiming to be a witch, had found her way to their notoriously ugly coven. Voicing their concerns to Carlotta, they devised a plan that would transform Minerva into a hideous witch before the Halloween night festivities began.

On a night soon thereafter, gathered around the fire, incanting words of evil and mischief, the witches began preparations for the initiation ritual. Each witch was given a vial of magic herbs, roots, and leaves which they poured into a bubbling cauldron wreathed in a swirling black mist. A long–handled cup was dipped into the pot, filled with the vile green potion, then passed to Minerva.

She gazed at the brew in horror and thought of running as fast as she could away from the campsite, but she realized the witches would overtake her and the punishment would be severe; there was no escaping.

With the witches forming a circle around her, chanting and watching intently, she closed her eyes tightly and gulped down the dreadful concoction. Poor Minerva! Her cup contained a sleeping potion, and she immediately fell into a deep sleep. The witches looked on in gleeful anticipation of the evil deed as Carlotta produced a pair of shears and a pot of ashes. The scissors were passed around the circle and each witch cut a blonde curl from Minerva's head until all her curls had disappeared.

With her short–cropped hair, Minerva looked like Peter Pan, but was still lovely to behold. The witches looked at her in disbelief. How could it be? Ah, but they knew the ashes would do the trick, so they smeared them all over her delicate skin. When they were finished, they clapped their hands and cackled, convinced they had, indeed, transformed Minerva into a hideous witch worthy of initiation into their infamous coven.

Minerva awakened to find her curls gone and her face covered with black ashes. Looking at her reflection in a pool, she found it hard to believe that her sister witches could be so cruel to one of their own. As she stared ruefully at her image, Minerva resolved that her comrades would suffer the consequences of their wicked actions.

Carlotta had determined that Minerva would be the last of the group to fly out on Halloween night. That way, she reasoned, they would frighten all the little kids to death before they saw Minerva. Even with her shorn hair and black face, she had a fragile, angelic, un–witchlike appearance.

Halloween night Minerva remained hidden until the last witch rode out. Her fair skin was completely devoid of the ashes and her cropped hair was covered by her witch's hat, adorned with lace and red roses, with a glittering halo attached at the very top. Her broomstick was shiny with sequins, and her black cape lined with star–studded spangles.

Once the witches made an appearance in the skies on that moonlit night, little children peeking toward the heavens began to cry and hide behind their mothers' skirts. Finally, when they found the courage to again look upward, little eyes grew wide with delight and excitement. They began to clap their hands and jump up and down as Minerva sailed high above them in the sky riding her sequin–studded broom.

The children were never again frightened by evil witches on Halloween night, because they knew that once the bad witches left, Minerva would appear all aglow in the night sky, casting a magical spell as she hovered high above the treetops. Her silvery image in the heavens gave the appearance of a shooting star with a shimmering halo, slightly askew, atop her witch's hat.

MOVE OVER, DOLLY

Ruth Crenshaw

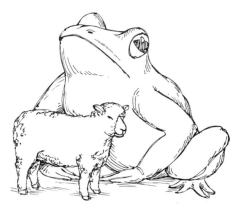

THOMAS Uriah Shaver and Harry "Twitch" Simpkins (a twitch in his right eye had earned him the nickname) had been hired as environmental technicians, or in plain English, janitors, at the Genetic Engineering Technology Laboratories—GET as it was called. Dr. Francis Bellingham, director of the laboratory, had interviewed them himself. Their supervisor, a Mr. Dinglespiel, laid down the rules for their employment. They were to clean and police certain areas, stay clear of the areas marked "Keep Out," and always wear their ID badges and their uniforms with the masks, caps and gloves. Without excuse, they were to abide by the strict rules of waste disposal: everything sorted into separate containers, even the sweepings from the vacuum, and placed in bins with weighted lids, then stored in a locked room to await removal by a special detail. Any infraction of these rules would bring immediate dismissal.

Since moving to the quiet community of what had once been a rather prosperous area of small truck farms, GET had given an economic transfusion to the almost forgotten town of Friendship whose lifeline had been severed by the interstate three years ago. Those farms not engulfed by the highway were now sold for a handsome price to the giant laboratory. Some locals, though classified as scientifically unskilled, were hired for the construction of the plant and its adjoining complex of homes for employees. Everyone wondered and gossiped about what was going on in that place. Some were afraid and felt the experiments were against God and nature. However, most appreciated the fact that the publicity surrounding Dr. Francis Bellingham and GET Laboratories was putting Friendship on the map. Long black limousines were frequently seen on the street (there was only Main Street) bearing men in business suits who bought gas, asked directions, and shopped for supplies at the General Store. Even Mrs. Waverly had taken to laying in a supply of strong drinks on the back shelves of her One Stop.

Then in 1995, Dr. Bellingham made international news by being invited to the Conference in California, where the leading scientists of the world were to meet to discuss the hazards of genetic engineering including cloning. The media crews swarmed in like locusts. Both Uriah and Twitch hung around, always at the front of the crowd, hoping to be interviewed by reporters making daily trips out to GET. With all the news surrounding the event, not one leak gave a real clue as to what research or experiments were being carried on in the sprawling buildings. One man said that GET was changing genes (whatever they were) and shipping them around the country. Uriah's curiosity was stirred even more, for that was his natural bent. He felt sure he could ferret out the secrets if only he could get inside the place. Now, after answering an ad posted in the barber shop, here he and Twitch were, inside!

The two young men had known each other only briefly in school. Uriah had graduated, or at least through his wily ways had conned himself a diploma. Twitch, however, had dropped out in the ninth grade when his parents, after selling their farm, had moved with his four brothers and two sisters to Bradford, leaving him to care for Aunt Ida, his mother's elderly sister. While working briefly as carpenters' helpers at GET, he and Uriah had become re–acquainted.

They were a most unlikely pair to become friends. Physically they were exact opposites. Uriah was rather short and muscular. He had regular features, an olive complexion, and piercing brown eyes. With his dark curly hair which clung in tight ringlets on his forehead, you might say he resembled an Etruscan icon. Twitch, on the other hand, was tall, about six feet–one, fair with thin yellow hair and watery blue eyes. The tic in his right eye was his one distinguishing feature. He had a sharp nose, exaggerated by his receding chin. Knobby joints and long arms contributed to his ambling gait when he walked.

Mentally they were also an unequal pair. Uriah had a quick mind for gleaning information from others. He seldom read anything. He had a glib tongue, and all through school he acted as class spokesman, sometimes with wit. He was a social being, girls made over him, but few adults trusted him. His parents. especially his mother, indulged him long past childhood. She called him her beautiful boy. His father secretly called him the smartest, most conniving liar he had ever known. Most of his teachers accepted his ability to fast–talk and seldom believed his excuses for poor homework preparation.

He made passing grades through his motto, "When in doubt, look about" and he always managed a seat by an A student. He went off to college, but was dismissed for damage to the chemistry building when he decided to try the forbidden experiment of mixing carbon, sulfur and potassium nitrate together.

Twitch was the slow-witted one of the pair. He would listen intently, but with a glazed, quizzical expression. He never seemed to have an original thought, which made him easily swayed by anyone, and Uriah was like a magician with Twitch in suspended animation. He would have followed Thomas Uriah Shaver anywhere. This fed Uriah's ego, and he took Harry "Twitch" Simpkins under his manipulative wing.

They seemed to work well together at GET. Twitch did most of the work, Uriah directed. While Twitch pushed the mop down long corridors, Uriah kept his ears peeled and his gimlet eyes open. The trouble was, no one talked in the corridors, and he was thwarted in the dining room where tables were assigned and the scientists ate in a separate room.

One day a break came in what was fast becoming a tiresome routine to Uriah. He was asked to help clean and move books onto new shelves in the library. He had made a special point of being friendly, always speaking to everyone and this assignment gave him another chance to ingratiate himself further. While moving the stacks of books with such titles as *Biofuture*, *Confronting the Generic Era*, and *Dealing with Genes*, he spotted a manual laying open on a table. The words CLONE and DNA jumped out at him. Quickly he slipped the book into the deep pocket of his coveralls. He couldn't believe his good fortune!

On the drive home after work, Uriah reported everything he had done and heard that day and proudly tossed the manual over for Twitch to see. He now knew what GET planned for those barrels of mud and pond water Mr. Beck had delivered to the plant. As sure as anything, they were building an artificial pond in the back wing, for the manual contained a step–by–step procedure for cloning FROGS. Into Uriah's cunning brain a plan was forming. Now his janitorial duties took on a new significance and excitement. After dinner he and Twitch met at Annie's Place to lay out details of his plan.

Twitch wanted to know about DNA and what cloning meant. Patiently Uriah explained that DNA was like a picture of a person in every cell of the body, even some of the blood. And cloning—well, that was producing a plant or animal without going through the usual way of being born or hatched.

"You know, like that lamb they named Dolly. The one they made over in Scotland," Uriah said, speaking with such authority that Twitch's mouth hung open in sheer amazement.

"GET is planning to make some frogs that way," he continued. "Shoot, Twitch, if we can get hold of some of those frog eggs that were shipped in from that place up north, I'll bet we could grow some bigger and quicker than any of those smart scientists. Who knows more about frogs than us country boys! Are you game, Twitch?"

Twitch still wore that glazed look after the explanation, but nodded as if he understood and assured Uriah he was all for the plan. "But, what if they ketch us?" he balefully asked.

"Don't worry," Uriah assured him. "They won't."

On Saturday Uriah made a visit to Mr. Beck and told him he wanted to build a pond in his back yard for the extra fish he usually caught.

"Take all the water and mud you need," Mr. Beck generously offered. "Just haul away."

From scrap lumber they built the lean-to rooms to serve as the laboratories. They added discarded windows in the roofs which they could open and close. Bit by bit, they collected other equipment. From the General Store they purchased two large tubs used for watering troughs, hauled four barrels of pond water and two of mud, taking care to harvest some water lilies, plenty of pond scum, mosquito larvae, and as many water skimmers as they could capture. They worked feverishly, and by the next Monday they were ready for the final stages of the plan.

The trickiest and most crucial part of Uriah's plan was to remove some of the frog eggs which had been delivered two days ago by special van to GET. They waited the five days for the unfertilized frog eggs to be injected with female's DNA. Then they made their move! It was easy to fool the guard on the front gate with the manual Uriah had snitched, with the excuse it must be replaced in the library. Twitch had brought a thermos of coffee for old man Moss, security guard in the wing where they worked.

Willingly the old man opened the library for Uriah. "Just pull it shut when you're through," he cautioned. While Twitch watched the monitors, old Moss sat back to enjoy the coffee. "That's not made by the gallons," he chuckled.

Quickly Uriah re–pocketed the manual he would need and closed the library door. He rushed to his equipment room, picked up two orange coolers marked BIO MATERIAL stacked in his oversized mop bucket and hurried to the back wing with its ponds and artificial climate. He was surprised at the ease with which he unlocked the heavy door. Mosquitoes swarmed as he carefully scooped up a few eggs from the small pond marked both in Latin and common name, *Bull Frogs*, and deposited them in one of the orange coolers.

In the next pond he found green tree frog eggs. "That's for me," he said to himself as he repeated the procedure. In less than ten minutes he was out of the pond wing and to the front door where he deposited the two coolers with their special cargoes. He called to Twitch and Mr. Moss. The old man accepted his explanation that someone was going to get in trouble over those coolers, which Uriah said he found in a corner of the equipment room.

"I'll just put them in my car and bring them back tomorrow to be properly discarded," he told the old man. "Don't put it in your report, or someone will get a pink slip."

The front gate guard accepted the same explanation and laughed when Uriah joked, "Oh, I thought I'd take a little of that DNA home to show to my mother."

They were home before Twitch drew a complete breath, and to Uriah their triumph was like drinking two large beers.

"We did it! We did it!" he chortled, slapping Twitch on the back. They deposited the bull frog eggs in Twitch's pond, and Uriah gave him final instructions: "Don't let them get too cold or too hot. Keep the lab door locked and don't breathe a word to anyone."

For three weeks both Uriah and Twitch slept in their laboratories, and spent every spare moment watching the tadpoles develop. Twitch had heard somewhere that if you kept frogs in an aquarium you could feed them spinach and boiled lettuce. So, along with Vitamin D, A, E, and C cocktails, he added spinach to their diet. Uriah added chicken wire over his pond for he knew that the adult tree frog can jump six to ten feet. He didn't want his Greenies—his code name for them—jumping through the window in the roof.

The sharp jangle of the telephone in the makeshift building caused Uriah to jump out of his reverie. Actually, he had been fantasizing the fame he was sure to be thrust upon him. It was Twitch on the phone.

His voice, pitched at least two octaves above normal, came screaming through. "Uriah, you gotta get here quick! Something strange has happened to the Bullies." That was his code name for his experiment. "Oh, my God, Uriah, you've just gotta see this—" His voice trailed off as he apparently let the receiver drop.

"Hello! Hello, Twitch, take it easy. Slow down! Hey are you there? What's happening?"

" Oh rats," he thought, "I guess I'll have to go down there and hold his blankity–blank hand and see what's got the dimwit in such a snit. He has a blooming seizure at the least little thing."

Now here he was, driving through a storm which had suddenly materialized to see what was wrong with Twitch's bull frogs.

He was getting more and more frustrated by the minute. First, the car wouldn't start, then the rain came down in sheets, and he couldn't see because the wipers had quit. Now the engine sputtered and died. He was out of gas!

He got out of the car and slogged his way through the mud. When he reached Twitch's he found the door wide open. He called, but there was no answer. The telephone receiver was dangling, but there was no Twitch. Down the street blue lights were flashing on the sheriff's patrol car. He could hear shouts and someone screaming. On the lab floor were pools of muddy water, Twitch's sneakers and his heavy brass belt buckle. Giant frog footprints led to the door, but still no Twitch! Panic, an emotion new to Uriah, gripped him. He was caught in one of those dreams we sometimes have which are more real than real.

Uriah woke from his nightmare in a cold sweat. His clothing was soaked, and he was seized with uncontrollable shaking.

"I've gotta call Twitch this minute and tell him to throw those tadpoles out," his brain shouted. As he reached for the telephone, it rang with the same loud jangle as in his dream.

It was Twitch. "Uriah, you gotta git here quick. Something strange is happening to the Bullies. You won't believe this," he screeched through the receiver.

Suddenly, Uriah's usual confidence returned. He no longer shook, and the warning shout from his brain was being replaced by what he thought was a brilliant scheme.

"Twitch, listen to me! Calm down and do as I tell you. Hang up now. Lock your door and don't let nobody in. Nobody! Do you hear me? I'm coming right down there."

Slowly Uriah checked his pond where his cute little Greenies were darting about. He was pleased that his experiment was progressing so smoothly. Already some of the tadpoles had shed their tails. Adding the grow light had definitely speeded up their development. He locked the door and looked up at the sky where streaks of lightning cut through heavy clouds as distant thunder rolled.

"Just like in that dream," he told himself. He began a tuneless whistle as he drove down the dirt road. "If that nightmare comes true, by the time I get there, old

Twitch will be long gone," he thought with a slight pang of remorse.

"Yep," he said out loud, "move over, Dolly, and make room for the dangedest bull frog there ever was. Yes, sir, Thomas Uriah Shaver, you may become famous after all! I'll sure see that a statue is built for good old Twitch."

LULA BETTERBEE'S CHRISTMAS TREE

Anne H. Norris

HAVING joined the staff of *The Star Gazette* only two weeks earlier, I was excited when the editor himself called me into his office. "Annie," he said, "I think this is a story right down your alley. Check out this old lady and see if she is as eccentric as her neighbors claim."

I was uncertain whether I should feel complimented or insulted to be given this assignment. I was pleased that he had remembered my name, but he had said this story should be "right down by alley." Was he implying that I, too, was an eccentric old lady?

I muttered a weak, "Thank you, Mr. Pauley. I'll get right on it." I grabbed a city map, along with my note pad, camera and purse, and was on my way.

Mr. Pauley, a man of few words, had not given me much information. He said he had been getting calls from the lady's neighbors, complaining about her Christmas decorations and her nightly ritual of burning sparklers in her front yard. She had discontinued the fireworks

235

after the second visit by the police, who had warned that they would be taking her in if she shot off another skyrocket. Still the neighbors complained that her behavior was degrading to their cove.

As I left the parking lot, I glanced again at the slip of paper Mr. Pauley had given me. All that was written on it was "Mrs. Lula Betterbee, 1805 Muy Bonita Cove." I had never been in that part of the city. It was what was referred to as "Out East"—certainly out of my modest neighborhood.

From my high school Spanish, I knew that "Muy Bonita" meant "very pretty," and the name certainly was appropriate. I gasped when I turned into the cove. All the houses seemed to be nestled in a pink and white forest with dogwood and redbud trees in full bloom. Azaleas—white, pink and shades of lavender—turned the entire cove into a fairyland. Lawns were perfectly manicured. The beauty of it all left no doubt that the people who lived on Muy Bonita Cove took great pride in their property.

It was not difficult to spot Number 1805. It was not that Mrs. Betterbee's lawn and spring flowers and trees were not as beautiful as those of her neighbors. It was the Christmas tree in her front window that attracted immediate attention. With its blinking red and green lights and the shining star at the top, it definitely seemed out of place for the middle of April. The snowman wreath on the front door added to my nervousness as I rang the bell.

Mrs. Betterbee wasn't at all as I had pictured her in my mind. She was such a petite lady. Her once blonde hair, now almost white, framed her cherub–like face in soft curls. When I introduced myself, her eyes sparkled like the glitter on the pot of silk poinsettia that centered her hall table. She invited me inside, giving me a warm smile and a gentle pat on my arm.

"Oh," she said, "I know why you are here. You want to see my tree. Some of my neighbors think I'm a bit daffy. They are always complaining to the police or the mayor. I guess now they have called your paper, but I don't pay them any mind. Of course I did have to stop the fireworks, and they were so pretty. But the police said there is some kind of law against shooting off fireworks inside the city. I was always very careful with them, but the officers were not very understanding."

I stepped into the "front room" as she called it, and there stood the tree in all its glory. Underneath it were beautifully wrapped packages. Every nook and cranny of the room had been decorated as if Mrs. Betterbee might be expecting Santa Claus that very night. She flipped on the stereo and Christmas carols added the final touch to the holiday setting.

After the shock of it all began to wear off a bit, I remembered why I was there. "Is there a special reason you celebrate Christmas in mid–April?" I asked.

Mrs. Betterbee chuckled and said, "Oh, I celebrate Christmas all year long. This beautiful tree has been right here for more than five years."

She remembered it all so well. Bob and Janet were such a nice young couple. She had been their real estate agent and had sold them their first house. They had wanted to get moved in before Christmas, but the seller had some health problems and the closing was postponed several times.

It wasn't easy to get all the papers signed, but she had used her feminine charms and somehow she pulled it all together. They were settled in a week before Christmas and Mrs. Betterbee had stopped by with a little housewarming gift. She had admired their tree, lamenting that she had been too busy to get hers down from the attic. Since her children were busy with their own families and wouldn't be coming home that year, it was all right. She probably would just sort of skip Christmas for once in her life.

It was early Christmas Eve. She had answered the knock at her door and there they stood. "Where's your old plastic tree?" Bob had asked with a grin. "I'll set it up, and Janet can start decorating it while I go to the store for some steaks."

It had been such a wonderful evening. Now the tree and all the decorations served as reminders of that night and the kindness of the young couple who didn't want Christmas to bypass the realtor who had been relentless in her efforts to see that they would be able to spend Christmas in their new home.

Mrs. Betterbee turned to me with a smile. "I never use this room anyway except during the holidays. It would be a shame to take down the tree and pack it away for a year. Besides, I don't have a very good working relationship with Christmas trees."

She explained that her late husband had always set up their tree and circled it with strings of lights. Her only contribution was adding the many ornaments which they had collected during their travels. That first Christmas after he died, she had dragged the tree down from the attic and set it up herself. It had been a much harder job than she had anticipated, but when she lay back on the sofa at 2:00 a.m. to admire the finished product, she felt good. And tired! Two hours later she awoke with a start. There was her tree lying flat in the middle of the floor. She covered it with a sheet, pronounced it dead, and went to bed.

The memory of that experience had influenced her decision to leave the present tree in the front room, not to be taken down and carried to the attic year after year. She admitted, though, that this past Christmas she'd had a hankering for a second tree, a white flocked one for the den. She had bought a beautiful spruce and several cans of spray–on flocking. The weather was not cooperative. It was the day after Christmas when the rain finally ended. Not to be defeated, she had taken the tree out to her front yard and had given it a good flocking before putting it at curbside for garbage pickup.

Mrs. Betterbee's neighbors may think she is a bit strange, and maybe she is. But I like her. She has a great attitude, a lot of fortitude, and a marvelous sense of humor. What's more, she keeps the Christmas spirit alive all year—not only in her heart, but also in her front room.

ABOUT THE AUTHORS

RUTH CRENSHAW is a graduate of the University of Tennessee College of Nursing and attended the University of Memphis for pre-medical studies. She spent time in Indian Service and taught Psychiatric Nursing at U.T. while rearing four children. She was active in several organizations, serving as president of Le Bonheur Club and as hospital board member. She was Kiwani's Woman of the Year in 1967 for her work in the hospital's building fund campaign. She served as president of both the local and state Medical Society Alliances and helped found the Health Sciences Museum Foundation which established the History of Health Care exhibit, "From Saddlebags to Science," in the Memphis Pink Palace Museum. She contributed to the book by the same title. Her avocation is history and for seven years she has participated in the Artists in the Schools Program as a storyteller of medical history. She is active in the Salvation Army and has been a volunteer in all of the Wonders' Exhibits. Her hobbies are music, gardening, and birds; her loves are her five grandchildren.

ANN J. HUCKABA is a Tennessean whose varied career includes spending World War II in the Marine Corps as an aircraft control tower operator; schoolteacher, secretary, and a corporate vice-president in merchandising. She is a long time supporter of historic preservation and served for many years on the Historic Sites Review Board for the State of Tennessee Her interests include antiques and the decorative arts, and she is currently writing a book related to the subject. She has served as president of the Memphis Story Tellers' League for two years and in many other capacities during her time of membership.

ETHEL JOYNER was born in Augusta, Ga., but has lived in Memphis most of her life. She retired from city government, having served as Executive Secretary to 23 Municipal Court Judges over a 25 year period. She is currently enrolled in Professor Richard C. Wood's Creative Writing Class at McWherter Senior Citizens Center, as well as taking writing courses at the University of Memphis. She is actively involved as a volunteer at Theatre Memphis and is the editor of the newsletter for Stage Set, an auxiliary of Theatre Memphis. She is a member of The Poetry Society of Tennessee. Her favorite pastimes are travel, writing, and the theatre.

MADGE H. LEWIS, former owner of a Memphis travel agency, is married and has a son, a daughter, and three grandchildren. For thirty years she traveled extensively to foreign countries in connection with her work and in many instances escorted groups to the fascinating corners of the world. She assisted her husband, Hal S. Lewis, in writing "A Short History of the Memphis Park Commission" which is used as reference material and can be found in the Memphis and Shelby County Room of the Memphis Public Library. Other published works have appeared in Writers' International Forum, *Arizona Literary Magazine*, and *Dogwood Tales*. She has received contest awards from *ByLine* Magazine, Arkansas

Writers' Conference, Writers Unlimited, Arizona Authors Association, Mid-South Writers' Association, and Florida State Writing Competition.

FAYE L. LIVINGSTON grew up on a farm in Nebraska. In her twenties she married and had two sons. In McCook, Nebraska, she met her cherished friend Millicent about whom she has written in this anthology. The two boys grew up in ranch country in western Nebraska where she was employed at the local newspaper as society editor, proof reader and all–round gofer. After the empty nest syndrome, she went to New York City for training and became an International Representative for Welcome Wagon. This brought her to Memphis. After marrying in Memphis, she gave up the traveling life her position required and joined her husband in the business world of insurance and brokerage. Belonging to the Memphis Story Tellers' League, and later serving two years as its president, provided the momentum for her desire to write stories, as well as tell them.

ANNE H. NORRIS, a native of Memphis, has never lived more than a few miles from her place of birth. She is married to Felix A. Norris, a high school classmate. She has two sons, a daughter, and four granddaughters. She is a former member of the Ninety-Nines. Inc., an international organization of licensed women pilots founded by Amelia Earhart. She participated for several years in the Powder Puff Derby, all-woman transcontinental air race. She edited a weekly newspaper, *Shelby County News*, followed by 32 years with the International Association of Holiday Inns, Inc. Her extensive travels in connection with her position have taken her to 29 foreign countries. She and her husband have toured the entire United States. This experience provided her with the expertise she displays in her short stories in this anthology. She is a prolific writer with the ability to listen to a humorous incident and turn it into a memorable story.

MALRA TREECE, Ph.D., is a professor emeritus, The University of Memphis. Her poems are published in regional and national magazines. Her poems and short stories have won numerous first–place awards from The Poetry Society of Tennessee, Mid-South Writers' Association, Arkansas Writers' Conference, Arkansas Poets Roundtable, and the Ozark Creative Writers Conference. In 1988 she was honored as Poet Laureate of The Poetry Society of Tennessee; in 1995 as Poet Laureate of the World Congress of Poets; and in 1997, Prose Writer of the Year by Mid-South Writers' Association. She has published 12 collegiate textbooks in business communication. Her 13th book is to be released in November, 1997 by Prentice Hall.

Home, when **NELLE BRUNER WEDDINGTON** was a child, was the small town of Lynnville, TN. Life centered around her family, the school, and the Presbyterian Church. She graduated from Tennessee Technological University. She is married and has a daughter. Writing ambitions came early. In the 1970s the Methodist Publishing House published several of her children's stories; since then, more than thirty pieces have appeared in various magazines and papers. Her work has won awards in Mid-South Writers' Association, Ozark Writers' Conference, Arkansas Writers' Conference and other contests. She now resides in Memphis.

RITA BERNERO WEST was a native Memphian whose untimely death last year left a void among the members of Professor Richard C. Wood's Creative Writers' Group in which she had become active. "A Time of Sacrifices" had just won a first-place award in the 1996 Mid-South Writers' Association contest and, when asked if this story could be used at the 1997 spring luncheon of The Memphis Story Tellers' League, she expressed an interest in joining the organization. Her story was told as scheduled, but after her death. She was greatly missed but her work was enthusiastically received by an appreciative audience. She was also a talented poet and her humorous poem, "The Denial of Sue Ann," appears in this anthology. Rita was a retired Court Reporter, politically active, mother of a son and a daughter, and grandmother of two children. Her hobbies were oil painting and sketching. We are grateful to her family for permission to include her story and poem in *Lights Along the Way*.

ABOUT THE ARTIST

SARAH CRENSHAW MCQUEEN, who illustrated this book, earned her B.S. degree in Medical Art from the University of Illinois at Chicago. Before turning freelance, she was a medical illustrator at Henry Ford Hospital in Detroit and Lutheran General Hospital in Park Ridge, Illinois. She has done medical illustrations for The Campbell Clinic, Duke University, and numerous medical publishers and businesses. She is a professional member of the Association of Medical Illustrators and has won several awards. She lives near Milwaukee, Wisconsin with her husband, two daughters, a Scottish terrier, and a tortoise–shell cat.

ACKNOWLEDGEMENTS

*The following have contributed to the publishing
of this anthology through their generous gifts:*

Mrs. Erwin Blatter
*In honor and admiration of
Mrs. Sebra(Roberta)Evans*

Mrs. Charles L. Brewer
*In honor of Pauline Buckler Hancock
and Dorothy Jane Emerson*

Mrs. A. Hoyt Crenshaw
In memory of Andrew Hoyt Crenshaw, M.D.

Ms. Rose E. Gillespie
*In memory of my dear friend,
Ruth Graves Russell, a truly remarkable woman.
Her life was an inspiration to many people.*

Mrs. Harold Holbrook
In honor of Mrs. Ralph W. (Nicie) Day

Mrs. G. W. Huckaba
In honor of my dear husband Bill

Mrs. C. S. Huttula
*In loving memory of my mother
Mary Jane McColl*

Mrs. Harold S. Lewis
In honor of my two wonderful children,
Kitty Phelan Moak and Patrick H. Phelan, IV

Mrs. Henry Lindeman
In loving memory of my grandmother,
Mrs. Ruth Graves Russell

Mrs. Thomas E. Livingston
In memory of my husband Tom,
who was always my inspiration

Mrs. Felix Norris
In honor of my children,
Gary, Michael and Janet

Mrs. Jimmie Stevens
In honor of
Mrs. Ralph W. (Nicie) Day

General Membership Treasury *and*
The Blanche Pence Fund
of
The Memphis Story Tellers' League